PRAISE FOR *REDEEMING THE FEMININE SOUL*

"I love this book! It's raw, courageous, smart, and biblical—a tremendous resource for every woman striving to honor God in her femininity. I could see Julie grow with each chapter, and she has inspired me to grow too. You can't possibly read this book without being challenged."

—Dr. Juli Slattery, cofounder of Authentic Intimacy and author of *No More Headaches* and *Passion Pursuit*

"I've known Julie for nearly thirty years and have witnessed her consistent passion to reach others with the truth presented in Scripture. In *Redeeming the Feminine Soul*, she makes a powerful case for womanhood to a culture that's in danger of erasing gender distinctions. I hope many will consider her arguments and take them to heart."

—Lee Strobel, bestselling author of *The Case for Christ* and professor of Christian thought at Houston Baptist University

"Julie Roys recounts her journey toward a compelling, redemptive vision for womanhood. Her story is transparent. Raw. Thought-provoking. A fascinating read for those wrestling with the question of what it means to be female."

—Mary Kassian, author of *Girls Gone Wise* and professor of women's studies at Southern Baptist Theological Seminary

"In our present age of gender confusion—or even willful disregard of plain facts—Julie Roys's book cuts through the cultural fog with the brilliant beacon of God's Word. Though Roys is deeply theological at all the right points, she writes not as an ivory tower academic but a theologian from the front lines of life. With rare insight and courageous honesty, she tells her own story as a way of exploring what it means to be a woman according to inerrant Scripture. Roys's book eloquently reminds us of the timeless beauty that the Creator imparted to the feminine soul."

—Bryan Litfin, professor of theology at the Moody Bible Institute and author of *Getting to Know the Church Fathers*

"Julie Roys has done it, a tremendously well-crafted book on an essential topic. The nature of gender and sex difference as it has been understood throughout recorded history is suddenly under attack today, and Julie parses out the truth on the feminine side of the debate wi⟨...⟩nd insight. Every woman—especially twe⟨...⟩t."

—Glenn Stanton, director o⟨...⟩ at Focus on the Family and ⟨...⟩ *Confident Sons* and *Loving M*⟨...⟩

D1113860

"In this book, Roys enters some complicated and controversial spaces, courageously and transparently offering her own story as the context from which to consider her message. In a world of so many strong opinions about gender and faith, not all will find full agreement with Julie's conclusions—but all will, at the very least, be drawn to her empathetic tone. With well-formed conviction that casts no judgment on the reader, Julie thoughtfully invites a conversation so needed for our time. Please read this book. Better yet, grab a friend and wrestle through it together. You'll be better for it."

—SCOTT SAULS, SENIOR PASTOR OF CHRIST PRESBYTERIAN
    CHURCH IN NASHVILLE, TENNESSEE, AND AUTHOR
    OF *BEFRIEND* AND *JESUS OUTSIDE THE LINES*

"As one who has devoted his life to sharing the great riches of the Theology of the Body across denominational lines, it was thrilling to read Julie Roys's account of searching for the true meaning of our creation as male and female and finding it in this bold, biblical response to the sexual revolution. One cannot help but be inspired!"

—CHRISTOPHER WEST, BESTSELLING AUTHOR AND
    LECTURER ON THE THEOLOGY OF THE BODY

"For too long the picture of women offered by various camps within the church has been reactionary and flat. Now, finally, Julie Roys offers a rich and robust understanding of what womanhood is and what it means for the church. *Redeeming the Feminine Soul*'s vision of women is refreshing in being both timely and timeless."

—KAREN SWALLOW PRIOR, PhD, AUTHOR OF
    BOOKED AND *FIERCE CONVICTIONS*

"Beginning with her own journey out of brokenness and pain, through healing, to a fuller understanding of God's very good design for male and female, Julie Roys speaks boldly, skillfully, and courageously about God's design for women. Hers is a life-giving story, skillfully told, that will help every Christian woman in search of biblically-informed clarity in the midst of a profoundly confused culture. Praise God for every faithful older woman who, like Julie, embraces her call to teach what is good and train younger women to be faithful in the expansive work given uniquely to women."

—CANDICE WATTERS, WIFE, MOTHER,
    AND AUTHOR OF *GET MARRIED*

REDEEMING THE FEMININE SOUL

REDEEMING THE FEMININE SOUL

GOD'S SURPRISING VISION FOR WOMANHOOD

JULIE ROYS

NELSON
BOOKS

An Imprint of Thomas Nelson

Published in Nashville, Tennessee, by Nelson Books, an imprint of Thomas Nelson. Nelson Books and Thomas Nelson are registered trademarks of HarperCollins Christian Publishing, Inc.

Published in association with Alive Literary Agency.

Thomas Nelson titles may be purchased in bulk for educational, business, fund-raising, or sales promotional use. For information, please e-mail SpecialMarkets@ThomasNelson.com.

Unless otherwise noted, Scripture quotations are taken from the ESV® Bible (The Holy Bible, English Standard Version®). Copyright © 2001 by Crossway, a publishing ministry of Good News Publishers. Used by permission. All rights reserved.

Scripture quotations marked KJV are from the King James Version. Public domain.

Scripture quotations marked NIV are from the Holy Bible, New International Version®, NIV®. Copyright © 1973, 1978, 1984, 2011 by Biblica, Inc.® Used by permission of Zondervan. All rights reserved worldwide. www.Zondervan.com. The "NIV" and "New International Version" are trademarks registered in the United States Patent and Trademark Office by Biblica, Inc.®

ISBN 978-0-7180-8780-7 (eBook)

Library of Congress Cataloging-in-Publication Data

ISBN 978-0-7180-8779-1
Names: Roys, Julie, 1965- author.
Title: Redeeming the feminine soul : God's surprising vision for womanhood / Julie Roys.
Description: Nashville, Tennessee : Nelson Books, an imprint of Thomas
 Nelson, [2017] | Includes bibliographical references.
Identifiers: LCCN 2017006566 | ISBN 9780718087791
Subjects: LCSH: Women--Religious aspects--Christianity. | Christian
 women--Religiouos life.
Classification: LCC BT704 .R69 2017 | DDC 248.8/43--dc23 LC record available at https://lccn.
loc.gov/2017006566

Printed in the United States of America

17 18 19 20 21   LSC   10 9 8 7 6 5 4 3 2 1

Dedication: To the most amazing woman I have ever known—my mother, Linda McMillen Stern (1934–2003). You not only gave me life, but the most important gift any mother could give: a passion for Jesus and the truth. I miss you more than words can say.

Imagine yourself as a living house. God comes in to rebuild that house. At first, perhaps, you can understand what He is doing. He is getting the drains right and stopping the leaks in the roof and so on; you knew that those jobs needed doing and so you are not surprised. But presently He starts knocking the house about in a way that hurts abominably and does not seem to make any sense. What on earth is He up to? The explanation is that He is building quite a different house from the one you thought of—throwing out a new wing here, putting on an extra floor there, running up towers, making courtyards. You thought you were being made into a decent little cottage: but He is building a palace.

—C. S. Lewis, *Mere Christianity*

CONTENTS

FOREWORD   xi

INTRODUCTION   xvii

ONE   EXCLUDED FROM THE BOYS CLUB   1

TWO   BROKEN, CODEPENDENT,
AND SURPRISINGLY FEMININE   15

THREE   SEX, SEXISM, AND SACRAMENT   31

FOUR   A MAN IN EVERY WOMAN AND
A WOMAN IN EVERY MAN   53

FIVE   ANDROGYNY, THE NEW MISOGYNY   69

SIX   BEYOND FEMINISM   83

SEVEN   GENDER CONSTRUCTION AND
CONFUSION   105

EIGHT   REDEMPTIVE SUFFERING   125

NINE   MARGINALIZING MOTHERHOOD   141

TEN   THE GLORIOUS BECOMING   169

ACKNOWLEDGMENTS   185

ABOUT THE AUTHOR   189

APPENDIX   191

NOTES   193

FOREWORD

By Kay Arthur

Like many Americans, I grew up in a Christian home and attended church every Sunday. I knew the Ten Commandments. I was baptized and confirmed and, because of that, the church told me I was a Christian. And I believed them. But I didn't know God—and I found His Bible hard to understand and boring.

As a result, I had no clue about what God said regarding women and our role, nor about marriage. My parents had a great marriage, so all I had to do was do what they did—or so I thought.

At the age of twenty, I walked down the aisle of the church to become Mrs. Frank Thomas Goetz, Jr. Physically I was a virgin, but mentally I was a harlot. Tom was twenty-one with a resume of outstanding achievements. But he was also bipolar, and neither of us knew it. On our honeymoon he sat me down and said, "You are now Mrs. Frank Thomas Goetz, Jr., and these are the things I don't like about you and want changed." Bubble burst!

After six years of marriage and two sons, I went to two ministers for counseling. Neither opened the Bible or prayed; they simply told me to leave Tom. Leave I did, and like the country western song I began "looking for love in all the wrong places." I threw away my convictions one by one, going from man to man and all the while sinking deeper into the pit I was digging with my own hands. When I found out the man I loved was married and had six kids, I didn't care! Our affair lasted for two years.

I had surrendered everything I once believed and valued for that man's love. I wasn't the mother I needed to be to the sons I loved dearly because I wasn't the woman God ordained me to be.

As I often say, *sin will take you further than you want to go, keep you longer than you wanted to stay, and cost you more than you ever intended to pay.* Eventually, *illicit love*—love and affections out of control, not kept within the security fence of God's commandments, His precepts—exacts a tremendous toll on one's soul. I didn't know that then. I was ignorant of the truths so clearly revealed in God's Word. If I had, I would have handled everything differently—my marriage, my motherhood, my sexuality.

Graciously, at the age of twenty-nine, God brought me to the end of myself. On July 16, 1963, I ran to my bedroom and cried out to Him, *God, I don't care what you do to me—if I never have another man in my life, if you paralyze me from the neck down, whatever you do to my two boys—please, just give me peace.* And He gave me the Prince of Peace, the Lord Jesus Christ. Immediately I felt washed clean and an overwhelming peace enveloped me.

God also sent me a godly young man who gave me a Phillip's translation of the New Testament, where I read, "And He called her beloved when there was nothing lovely about her." The Spirit of God had moved in, the veil over His Word was removed, and I fell in love with the Word of God and the God of the Word!

Wanting to please God, I told him that I would go back to my first husband. But before I could do so, Tom committed suicide. A couple of years later God, in His immense mercy and divine timing, brought me Jack Arthur, a stable, solid man of God. We married and went as missionaries to Mexico for three and a half years, where I began teaching teenagers how to dig into God's Word.

One day, a deep sadness over my past overwhelmed me. *Why hadn't God saved me sooner? Why did my older sons have to have two daddies when they should have had one? Why couldn't they have had a better mother?* As I sat in the rocking chair nursing David, my newborn, I asked God through tightened lips, *God, why when I was young, and before I had messed up my life, didn't you send somebody to teach me the things I am now teaching these teenagers?*

I'll never forget the words as God spoke them to my heart, "I saved you when I wanted to save you. And if you'll quit moaning and groaning about your past, and share it, I'll use it."

That's what I've been doing for the past five decades. God has redeemed so much. He's given me a wonderful family and a ministry that by His grace continues to touch millions. But I still have a strong passion to warn women not to make the tragic mistakes I made and to teach them the transformational truths revealed in God's Word. That's why I'm so excited about Julie's book.

Redeeming the Feminine Soul is not a typical book on womanhood. I know the Word of God. I've written an inductive study on marriage for men, women, and even teens. I've written a book on marriage. I'm now eighty-three, and I've been around the block with all the feminist issues. And yet I devoured Julie's book.

I didn't want to put it down. I marked it up and wrote notes along with page numbers on the title page so I could go back and digest Julie's rich insights and get them into my head in order to share what I had learned from her. I've marveled at the research on women Julie uncovers, and chuckled as I have considered the wisdom of the One who ordained our womanhood.

The culture may change; our Creator does not. I've grieved over the men and women who have bought Satan's lie, thinking they've been liberated, believing they know more than God and can get away with twisting or breaking His commandments, when in reality they go into greater bondage.

Julie's writing has blown on the hot embers of His truth in my heart and set them so afire that I want every woman to read *Redeeming the Feminine Soul*. At my age, it's not often I read something—especially about women's issues—that teaches me something new. But I was amazed by Julie's book. She shares so much credible research that shows you why our Creator lays down the parameters He does. There is nothing new under the sun!

I meet so many women, even Christian women, confused about their identity, their callings, and how to navigate life's many choices. Julie's research, coupled with biblical truth, has equipped me to better guide these women, and to communicate to them the liberation that can be ours—the peace, power, and victory we can experience when we live according to our Creator's Word.

I especially appreciate Julie's honesty and vulnerability throughout her book. She doesn't teach biblical truths in an academic way, but instead vulnerably tells her own, often very raw and unvarnished, story as a context for understanding these truths.

I firmly believe that when we're honest and willing to share with others what God has taught us, then the body of Christ is enlightened and strengthened. *Redeeming the Feminine Soul* is an invaluable, culturally-enlightening tool we all can use to help others discover God's precepts for life so they can rebuild their lives on the solid rock of truth. It's never too late with God!

How I pray God will use it to liberate women who have bought the lie of the "prince of this world" and are sabotaging their own womanhood.

Get prepared. Buy several copies for friends and family! You won't want to risk giving away the one you've marked up!

INTRODUCTION

"You all don't seem as emotional on this topic as I am," said Anita Lustrea, a respected colleague and cohost of *Midday Connection*, a discontinued program on the Moody Radio Network. Anita had been relatively quiet for much of the conversation, which wasn't like her. Normally she was quick to share her view and to engage with other women on hot-button issues, but this one hit especially close to home. "I realize that a lot of . . . my pain has come out of my family of origin and that whole idea that . . . men are better," she said. "Do whatever you can to be more like a man because you'll survive a lot better, especially if you're a Christian woman. I mean, how sad is that?"

Around the table we all groaned in knowing agreement. The six of us women, assembled to record two podcasts on women's roles, all came from similar church backgrounds but belonged to two different generations.[1] Three of the six of us were over forty—Anita; Melinda Schmidt, Anita's cohost on *Midday Connection*; and me. The other three were under thirty at the time—Katelyn Beaty, former managing editor of *Christianity Today*; Morgan Sutter, a graduate of Moody Bible Institute and an aspiring playwright; and Crystal Anderson, another Moody graduate and part-time employee of Moody Radio. The six of us had differing opinions on women's roles, but we had just found common ground. All of us agreed that we lived in a man's world and had to conform to get by. And all of us agreed that the topic of women's roles triggered strong emotions.

"I am very nervous about this topic," Crystal said—evidently not as dispassionate as Anita had assumed. "Just to let you know, on the inside, I'm actually shaking right now, which is really weird because I've been fine all day up until we sat down at the table and I was like, 'Oh my gosh, there's just—there's so many elements to this, and there's such a history, and emotions.'" Crystal, who had traveled to more than twenty countries as a personal assistant for an international leader, had witnessed horrific oppression of women firsthand. She had been in African villages where women were subjected to genital mutilation. She had stayed in Muslim communities where polygamy was practiced and women forced other women to submit to dehumanizing practices. "They treat [other women] like dirt," she said, "because they were treated like dirt." Crystal had grown up in a Christian home where she was taught that men should lead and women should submit. But, given what she had witnessed, could she really embrace that vision? She was conflicted.

"I can't believe that patriarchy is God's dream for the world," Morgan chimed in, quoting Sarah Bessey, author of a recent book called *Jesus Feminist*, which several of us had read.[2] In the Christian community where Morgan had grown up, *feminism* was a dirty word. But due to her negative experiences with men in the conservative church, Morgan viewed *patriarchy* as an even more odious word. Although embracing so-called Jesus feminism created conflict with her mother, Morgan openly did so. Feminism needs a makeover, she argued. Christians tend to think of feminism as militant or angry, she said, but Jesus feminism isn't either of these things. Then, quoting the subtitle of Bessey's book, Morgan said Jesus feminism is simply "the radical notion that women are people too"—or put another way, "the affirmation of the full personhood of women, and that's why I attach to that label."

Similarly Katelyn, who had interviewed Bessey for *Christianity Today*, also expressed an affinity for Jesus feminism—and for Bessey. "She is very personable," Katelyn said. "She's not a radical. She doesn't fit these stereotypes of what we might think of as a feminist. And I think that's very intentional. I think that will actually win more people to what she's trying to say about women's roles in the church and the kingdom of God." Katelyn added, "The idea that women are called . . . to fully participate in what God is doing in the world . . . that's a bottom-line commitment for me, and I think for her, as well."

Katelyn's conviction that women should fully participate in the kingdom of God resonated with me. I knew well the hurt that comes from being excluded or dismissed simply because I'm a woman—and so did each of the women participating in our discussion. Morgan said that what initially made her interested in Jesus feminism "was I got so tired of feeling like I had to fight for my place at a theological table. Or, I got so tired of trying to prove that my opinions were still valid. And, I would constantly be met with, 'Well, you're not going to be a pastor.' Or, 'But you're not going to lead a church.' Or, 'Why does this matter to you?' I have never wanted to be a pastor, or to lead a church. . . . I just wanted to think, and I just wanted to discuss, and I just wanted to feel like my discussion and my thoughts and my intelligence mattered—and I didn't have to be a man to have it matter."

Clearly, some of these women felt demeaned and disenfranchised and were longing for a better way than the chauvinism they had experienced in the church. But was Jesus feminism the answer? Several of the women thought so. And who among us could argue with the "notion that women are people too"? But was that really what those opposed to Jesus feminism believed—that women aren't people? I knew that wasn't the case. Despite their negative experiences in the church, and at times being treated as if they weren't equal persons, so did the women assembled around that table. The slogan was propaganda—brilliant in its ability to sway emotions and to vilify the opposition, but terribly misleading.

Both Jesus feminists and traditionalists agree that men and women are of equal worth, though admittedly, traditionalists sometimes fail to act that way. Where these two camps disagree is on the purposes and functions of men and women. Traditionalists, or *complementarians*, assert that God designed men and women for different, or complementary, purposes and functions. But Jesus feminists, or *egalitarians*, argue that women and men have essentially the same purpose and function. Although Bessey, the chief proponent of this new feminism, tried to distance herself from the feminist stereotype, her book essentially embraced the major tenets of secular feminism: (1) women are free to define themselves, and (2) men's and women's roles are interchangeable. These were truly radical notions—at least for conservative Christians.

As someone who doesn't necessarily fit the traditional stereotype of biblical womanhood, I can understand why these notions appeal to Christian women. Plus there's no denying that feminism has achieved much for women, especially in business and education. Over the past forty years, women have gone from earning 59 percent of a man's median salary to 76 percent of it.[3] Women are also now more likely than men to have bachelor's degrees,[4] and we earn more master's degrees and doctoral degrees than our male counterparts.[5]

But strangely we are less happy now than when feminism went mainstream, according to a key study by economists Betsey Stevenson and Justin Wolfers. They found that in the 1970s, women actually rated their overall life satisfaction higher than men. Since then women's happiness scores have steadily declined. By the 1990s men surpassed women on the happiness scale and have remained happier ever since.[6] If feminism is the answer to women's problems, why hasn't it made us happier?

We discussed some of the drawbacks of feminism as a group but didn't really come to any conclusions. Several were bothered by the movement's association with abortion,[7] though some argued that Christians could embrace parts of feminism without embracing the whole. Toward the end of our time, Melinda astutely observed, "It's interesting that women are aching for something. . . . There is a hole—sometimes a wound, even, that I think [*Jesus Feminism*] addresses. . . . Some women are very happy with whatever the church tells them, whatever their pastor tells them. Other women are feeling left out. Frankly, they're disturbed about how they are portrayed in the church. Would you agree?"

I did agree. And that ache, or hole, was palpable among the group of women assembled that day. Some had found solace by embracing feminism, while others were suspended between feminism and traditional womanhood. But no one seemed especially liberated. They seemed conflicted, frustrated, and hurt. Certainly, there must be something better for women. This was not the abundant life Jesus offered.

For the past thirty years, I have been searching for that abundant life, for a better vision of womanhood. If the pages of Scripture are true—and I firmly believe they are—then God has something deep, rich, and beautiful for women that we're missing. But what is it? And how can we appropriate His glorious vision for our lives? I don't pretend to have all the answers, nor am I a perfect model of biblical womanhood. But over the years I've had several epiphanies.

Some of these have come through studying Scripture or reading great Christian thinkers. Others have been produced in the crucible of brokenness and on the journey to healing.

Sometimes struggle can be a blessing. A teacher once explained to me that she was a good teacher not because the subject matter came easily to her, but because she had struggled so much to grasp the subject that she could relate to similar strugglers and show them how to overcome common obstacles. In many ways that describes my relationship with the topic of this book: I have struggled with womanhood and my place as a woman in God's family. But I am grateful for that struggle because it has produced understanding and experiential knowledge that have borne much fruit in my life.

So if you struggle with womanhood, or simply want a deeper understanding of God's design for women, I invite you to journey with me. There is something better for women—something much better.

ONE

EXCLUDED FROM
THE BOYS CLUB

I sat in a large, corporate-looking church auditorium, surrounded mostly by men. I shifted uneasily, crossing and uncrossing my legs, and then stared at the high vaulted ceiling. I honestly didn't know if I could bear another message that would only fan the flames I believed would be better extinguished. I shared a knowing glance with my husband before the speaker began. He clearly felt my angst but was at a loss as to how to help. He half-smiled and squeezed my hand. I sighed and sank into the lavender upholstered seat.

The message was what I expected: a call to pursue God without reservation, to diligently study His Word, and to boldly preach the gospel to a lost and dying world. I passionately wanted to do all those things. But as a woman in a conservative evangelical church, that was a problem. Scripture, my church maintained, strictly prohibited women from preaching.

I'm not sure why my pastor had invited our entire staff, both men and women, to attend our denomination's pastors' conference. The messages were clearly designed for men. Women in our church could teach only other women and children, which was arbitrarily defined as anyone under eighteen. As youth pastors at our church, that's precisely what my husband and I had been doing. But I longed to do more. I especially wanted to preach. I had messages inside me that burned to be expressed. The pastor shared the pulpit with all the men on staff, some of whom clearly lacked communication skills. He also invested time training them to exposit Scripture, something I desperately wanted to learn. But because of my sex, I was disqualified.

I also longed to give input on the direction of the church. After working several years with the youth, I saw ways the church was unknowingly alienating the teenagers and young adults in our congregation. But seldom was my opinion ever sought or considered. Instead, almost all decisions at our church were made by an all-male elder board, along with our senior pastor and assistant pastor, both of whom were men. They were godly people, and I truly respected each one of them. But as a woman serving in the church, I felt completely disenfranchised by this all-male club.

There had been a time when I thought things might change. Our pastor asked the entire staff to read a book on leadership and then come to a meeting ready to discuss it. I was extremely excited about this assignment, thinking it might finally give me an opportunity to discuss my thoughts about ministry with our pastors. I devoured the book and had three pages of notes suggesting how we might apply the book's principles to the church. But at our so-called discussion, our senior pastor simply quizzed the staff to determine whether we had read the book, and then moved on to other business. I was so angry. I felt invisible.

A SERIES OF BLOCKED DREAMS

As a woman serving in the conservative church, I had come to expect these kinds of slights and blocked opportunities. In high school I was part of a group that started a Christian coffeehouse to reach out to non-Christians in my community. I spent practically every free moment serving the ministry in one way or another and shouldered more responsibilities than any other young person in our group. Yet when it came time to appoint a student leader to the ministry board, a young man was chosen. Somewhat apologetically, one of the adult leaders explained to me that they had no choice. Even though the board recognized that functionally I was serving as the leader, biblically a man was needed to hold that position. I didn't care about the title, but the whole system seemed incredibly disingenuous.

Soon after graduating from college, I felt a strong call to the ministry. I had experienced a dramatic spiritual rebirth and had played a key role in leading several coworkers, and their friends and families, to faith in Christ. Kingdom work captured my imagination, and I couldn't think of anything I wanted to do more than pastor and preach.

Though women pastors were extremely rare in my conservative Christian circles, they weren't unusual in my family. My great-aunt had been an evangelist and church planter in the Wesleyan Church. Thanks to her, my grandfather, who was raised in an abusive alcoholic home, came to faith in Christ and eventually served as a medical missionary in Sierra Leone, West Africa. My grandmother, who taught Bible at Houghton College, had actually met my grandfather while preaching with my great-aunt in evangelistic crusades in the poor areas of Appalachia in western New York. My mother served as superintendent of Sunday school for my childhood church. She also knew Greek and had a degree from Fuller Theological Seminary. So joining the pastorate didn't feel foreign or unnatural; it was simply what women in my family did.

However, the Wesleyan Church of my mother's side of the family was an anomaly among theologically conservative churches, especially in the late eighties and early nineties. When I moved from the East Coast to the Midwest to attend college, most of the conservative churches I encountered did not permit women to preach or pastor. Even in the churches that did, there was an underlying aversion to women in those roles for various reasons.

When I expressed my desire to pastor to my former boss—a man my husband and I had led to the Lord—he responded that he felt men were best equipped to pastor churches. Similarly, when my husband and I explored putting together a team to plant a church, even those with no theological objections to women pastoring expressed reservations. Men simply won't follow a woman, I was told. As a result my husband, Neal, felt tremendous pressure to lead a church-planting team. Team pastoring was acceptable to most of the people we knew, so if Neal pastored, then I could serve alongside him. But Neal didn't want to pastor. He loved serving in the church but felt called to teach in the local public school and was thriving in that role.

This blocked dream and lack of affirmation left me terribly confused. Before experiencing these disappointments, I had planned to attend seminary and had been accepted at a leading seminary in the Chicago area. But since the job prospects for women in the church seemed so bleak, I decided instead to get a master's degree in broadcast journalism. For several years I worked in TV news. I loved the job, but I couldn't escape my passion and calling to ministry. So when my husband led several of his students to Christ and they began gathering in our home, Neal and I wondered if God might be calling us to youth ministry. We had one child at the time, and I was finding the demands of TV news and motherhood to be incompatible. So after several months of seeking God's will, we decided I would quit my job and we would search for a church in the area that would hire us as part-time youth ministers.

One church rejected us because they felt I was more the visionary leader between my husband and me. This made me the "point person," which was problematic because, in their estimation, teenage boys wouldn't follow a woman. Their response not only dashed our dreams of serving in their church, but it also made us wonder if there was something wrong with our marriage. Was Neal not a strong enough leader? Was I too strong of a leader? Or were we simply gifted differently and should just ignore their judgments?

We never arrived at a conclusion, but we eventually found a church plant that wanted to hire both of us to start a youth ministry there. In some ways I thrived at that church. The youth ministry quickly blossomed, and for the first time I had a title and a paycheck that actually acknowledged God's call on my life. But this acknowledgment was limited: once, when I confided in my assistant pastor that I longed to preach and even plant a church, he emphatically stated, "That takes a visionary leader, and you are not a visionary leader!"

Those demoralizing words played over and over in my head. To the pastor of one church, I was disqualified from service because I was too much of a visionary leader, but to the pastor of another, I was not a visionary leader at all. The continued mixed signals, lack of affirmation, and blocked dreams triggered an avalanche of self-doubt and confusion. Was I wrong to feel the way I did? Was this passion to preach and pastor just a manifestation of my pride and ego? Why couldn't I just be like other women, who seemed content with the roles they were assigned? Was there something fundamentally defective about me?

THE BOILING POINT

My inner turmoil came to a head at the pastors' conference. At each session the tension mounted more and more; by the final evening I was ready to explode. My mother once told me that she had met women in seminary whose calls to ministry were so strong—and the barriers to fulfilling those calls so impenetrable—that they thought they might have nervous breakdowns. That's precisely how I felt at the end of the conference.

At the close of the message on the final night, the speaker, a prominent pastor in our denomination, issued a specific invitation to receive prayer. His words so accurately named my situation that I felt as if he was speaking directly to me: "Some of you tonight know you have been called by God to a certain role or ministry, but you have never been blessed or affirmed in that calling. If that's you, I believe God wants to minister to you tonight."

His words instantly unleashed a torrent of emotion as all my pent-up angst flooded to the surface. *Why, Lord, why?* I cried silently. *Why would you put preaching and leadership gifts inside a female body? If you were going to make me this way, why didn't you just give me a Y chromosome? Why am I even here?*

I poured out all my anger, my doubts, and my frustration. My cries turned to sobs as I allowed my heart to spew everything it felt— and what I felt wasn't pretty. Honestly, in that moment, I didn't like being a woman at all. Some people talked about womanhood as a beautiful gift, but it certainly didn't seem like a gift to me. After two decades of dashed dreams, frustration, and angst, I had come to view womanhood not as a blessing but as a curse.

I hated being a woman.

SEARCHING FOR ANSWERS

If there was one thing I knew about the God of the Bible, it was that He was not capricious or cruel. He loved me and wanted what was best for me. Romans 8:28, one of the most popular verses in the Bible, affirms "that in all things God works for the good of those who love him, who have been called according to his purpose" (NIV). But I wondered, *how could a God who loves me make such apparently sexist rules, which made my life miserable?* This thought tortured me. Was God a misogynist? I couldn't bear that thought. I loved God and had devoted my life to Him. Yet, how could I reconcile this male-dominated system with a God who supposedly loved me and had created me the way He had? I searched for answers, reading books and articles on the topic and discussing it with other Christians who had done likewise.

Egalitarian scholars—those who believe men and women are equal in worth and equal in function—argue that male hierarchy is the result of the Fall. Initially God had created man and woman to live harmoniously as equals. But when God cursed Eve for her sin, He not only promised to increase her pain in childbirth, but also decreed, "Your desire will be for your husband, and he will rule over you."[1] So hierarchy, they assert, was not part of God's original intent but a tragic consequence of sin.[2] Yet, because Jesus conquered sin and death at the cross, this consequence could be reversed. In the community of those redeemed by Christ, relationships between men and women should revert to their harmonious pre-Fall state, and hierarchy should be eliminated.

I naturally gravitated to the egalitarian view. It made sense and offered a means of escaping the male-dominated system I found so oppressive. However, complementarian scholars—those who believe men and women are equal in worth but different (or complementary) in function—argue that God's curse against Eve did not establish male hierarchy.[3] According to them God established male hierarchy prior to the Fall as part of the created order described in Genesis 2. God created the man first and then the woman.[4] He also commanded the man not to eat from the tree of the knowledge of good and evil, leaving him with the responsibility of communicating this rule to the woman.[5] Adam's leadership, then, was not the result of sin but part of God's original design.[6]

Yet even within the complementarian camp, there exist two views concerning God's pronouncement in Genesis 3 that the man will rule over the woman. Similar to egalitarians, some view this pronouncement as part of the curse against women and a perversion of the relationship God intended between the sexes. Though God intended men to lead, they argue, He did not intend them to oppress and dominate. The cross then fundamentally changed the nature of male leadership—from the oppressive rule described in Genesis 3 to the kind of servant leadership Jesus modeled and advocated. As it says in Ephesians 5:25, husbands should love their wives "as Christ loved the church and gave himself up for her."[7]

However, other complementarians teach that God's pronouncement of rule is not a perversion of God-ordained leadership, but is actually a prescription of how male leaders should operate. As Rusty Lee Thomas writes in *The Kingdom Leadership Manual*, "God's command, 'he shall rule over you,' was intended to protect and provide for women and children."[8] To these complementarians, men ruling over women is a good thing. I've even heard some complementarians assert that since Eve was deceived first, women are more gullible than men and, for their own good, need their husbands to make their decisions for them.

I found this latter view extremely demeaning and offensive. There was no way I could embrace a view portraying such a low opinion of women. I found the other complementarian view palatable, but more of a theory than actual practice. Had I witnessed more servant leadership among men in the church, I might have been more open to it. As it was, male leadership felt a lot like "rule," and I had a natural aversion to it.

Even so, I discussed the issue numerous times with my senior pastor, hoping to gain some insight. He would often point to 1 Timothy 2:11–15:

> A woman should learn in quietness and full submission. I do not permit a woman to teach or to assume authority over a man; she must be quiet. For Adam was formed first, then Eve. And Adam was not the one deceived; it was the woman who was deceived and became a sinner. But women will be saved through childbearing—if they continue in faith, love and holiness with propriety. (NIV)

I hated those verses, but I couldn't deny that they seemed to prohibit women from teaching or leading men. Yet the passage seemed odd. Why would women be saved through childbearing? Some scholars actually argued that it meant women would be saved from dying in childbirth. Others said it pointed to Christ, the Savior of the world, being born of a woman. And still others said it meant that women should not violate their role by teaching and preaching, but should assume their proper place as the mother of children.[9] None of these interpretations seemed compelling or convincing to me. Plus, I questioned the wisdom of basing an entire doctrine on one dubious passage.

However, there were other passages that supported exclusive male leadership. My pastor often referenced 1 Corinthians 11:3 and

Ephesians 5:23, where Scripture refers to the husband as the "head" of the wife. This, he said, shows a God-ordained hierarchy in which the man leads and the woman follows. He also referenced 1 Timothy 3:2, where Scripture says an overseer should be "the husband of one wife," apparently assuming that all overseers would be male.

I could easily see how my pastor arrived at his conclusions. Yet his answers failed to satisfy my fundamental question as to why God would make these rules. When I pressed him and other Christian friends on this, they offered a pragmatic rationale: decisions are more efficiently made when there's a clearly defined authority. I replied that no one denies the efficiency of tyranny or oligarchy, but if we truly thought those best, then we'd all live in Cuba instead of the United States.

I didn't mind the concept of a benevolent dictatorship when God, someone all-knowing and good, sat on the throne. But when applied to men in general, benevolent dictatorship seemed at best a recipe for leadership that misunderstands the interests of women, and at worst a recipe that completely disregards them.

As I continued to press my pastor, he resorted to, "That's just what Scripture says." This answer was completely unsatisfying. It reminded me of a parent saying, "Because I told you so!" What I needed was a compelling rationale for why God would establish a system that seemingly disenfranchises half of the church, but I couldn't find one.

Not everyone agreed with these interpretations of key New Testament passages though. In fact, in *I Suffer Not a Woman*, scholars Richard and Catherine Clark Kroeger argued that the traditional interpretation of 1 Timothy 2:11–15 completely misses the apostle Paul's intention. For example, the passage's admonition for women to learn in "quietness and full submission" (NIV) was precisely the way men learned in Hebrew and Jewish cultures. Rather than discouraging women's participation in the church, the passage is encouraging it. They also argued that the Greek word *authentein*, which is translated in verse 12 as "to assume authority" (NIV), only occurs once in the entire New Testament and has a dubious meaning. It could mean "to dominate" or "to usurp authority." So the passage could merely be admonishing women not to assert a wrong kind of authority.[10]

The Kroegers also explain that at the time of Timothy's writing, many in the church had fallen prey to the false Gnostic teaching that Eve actually created Adam and made him wise by passing on the secret knowledge of good and evil. The authors argue that the apostle Paul wrote this passage specifically to address this false teaching, noting that *authentein* sometimes has the connotation of being an "author" or "originator." As a result, the passage might best be translated, "I do not allow a woman to teach nor represent herself as originator of man, but she is to be in conformity with the Scriptures. . . . For Adam was created first, then Eve."[11]

Egalitarian theologians also challenge the notion that "head" in 1 Corinthians 11 and Ephesians 5 means "leader" or "authority." In *Beyond Sex Roles* Gilbert Bilezikian, a professor with whom I studied in college, insisted that *kephale*, the word translated as "head," is better understood as "originator" or "source," as in the head of a river. So when Paul says the husband is the head of the wife, he doesn't mean the husband is the wife's leader. He means the husband is her source—that the husband nourishes and supports his wife.[12]

Of course, complementarians have good counterarguments for all these egalitarian arguments. For example, theologian Wayne Grudem notes that *head* in almost all ancient documents means either one's physical head or someone in authority, not "source." And in the few instances where *head* is used in conjunction with a river, it clearly means the end point of a river, not the river's fountainhead.[13]

Similarly, scholars such as Andreas J. Köstenberger, Thomas R.

Schreiner, and H. Scott Baldwin studied dozens of ancient documents where *authentein* was used. They concluded that the word almost certainly denotes some kind of authority, not "author" or "originator" as the Kroegers suggest in their book. Köstenberger, Schreiner, and Baldwin admit the word could be used negatively, as in "to control" or "to dominate," but the context suggests the most likely meaning is "to exercise (positive) authority over."[14]

CONFLICTED AND UNDECIDED

While perhaps not probable, the egalitarian interpretations were plausible enough for me to embrace them, at least on the surface. But I remained conflicted. When I was brutally honest, I had to admit that the egalitarian arguments seemed as if they were trying to explain away the obvious. Was there really no fundamental difference between men and women? And if not, why did God create two genders? Was it merely for procreation?

But the complementarian arguments led to such an odious system that I couldn't swallow them either. This camp seemed so focused on rules and roles that they missed women's basic humanity. Instead of blessing and embracing women as unique persons, they often related to us as a class, or even a subclass. Plus, they failed to communicate any real, positive vision for womanhood. Being a woman seemed all about what one couldn't do. But what about what we could do, perhaps even more competently and gloriously than any man?

The complementarians seemed to be missing the forest for the trees, but the egalitarians had razed the entire forest. Certainly God designed us male and female for something far better and richer than what I was experiencing. But despite years of searching, I still hadn't found it.

LIVING IN THE TENSION

As I sat at the pastors' conference sobbing, I desperately wanted to hear a word from God—something that would help me make sense of my call, my marriage, and more fundamentally, my womanhood. My assistant pastor's wife came and sat beside me and asked if I wanted to talk. Despite the fact her husband was part of a system that had hurt me, I told her about my struggle. She listened and didn't offer any advice, she simply offered to pray.

During that prayer time nothing dramatic transpired. I had hoped the heavens would open and God would descend with a revelatory message that would change everything. But He remained silent—and I remained stuck. I was hoping my struggle to understand and embrace my gender was ending, but it was just beginning. For years I lived with that tension, tentatively embracing an egalitarian vision of womanhood that seemed better than the alternative but not necessarily compelling or true. Then God turned my world upside down. Through a series of events I couldn't possibly have anticipated, He exposed areas of need I never knew I had. He showed me that my femininity is not merely stamped on my body; it is woven into the fabric of my soul.

TWO

BROKEN, CODEPENDENT, AND SURPRISINGLY FEMININE

Growing up, I thought mine was the model Christian family, and in many ways it was. My parents were pillars of our rural Pennsylvania community, maintaining high moral standards in both private and public. My father worked as a surgeon at the local hospital and had a sterling reputation. My mother was a stay-at-home mom and created a stable environment for my brother, two sisters, and me. Both my parents served as leaders in our church and enjoyed the respect of most everyone I knew. As for us kids, we weren't perfect—we fought and got in trouble and sometimes disobeyed our mom and dad—but for the most part we kept our noses clean and made our parents proud. We all graduated from Christian colleges, got advanced degrees, married Christian spouses, and eventually began raising families of our own. We appeared to be a Norman Rockwell family. As evidence of how much we enjoyed each other, we continued to vacation together every summer despite living hundreds of miles apart and maintaining busy family schedules.

Yet, it was during one of those family vacations that I first became aware of how flawed our seemingly perfect family was. I don't recall what sparked the conversation, but I vividly remember my brother—whom I have seen cry only a handful of times—sobbing as he recalled a decades-old event. Twenty-five years earlier, my parents had served as medical missionaries in Southern Rhodesia (now Zimbabwe). The moment my brother recalled was when my parents visited him for the first time since sending him to boarding school. He was only eight at the time, and he had desperately missed my parents. He described the day they visited as heaven, and when they got in the car to go, he melted down. He ran to the car, frantically clung to the driver's-side door, and started screaming, "Don't go! Don't go!" Other missionaries and children were present, and my brother's desperate display apparently made a scene. My dad told my brother he was embarrassing the family and ordered him to stop. When my brother didn't relent, my father reportedly slapped my brother's hands away from the car, scolded him harshly, and drove away.

My sisters and I were aghast when my brother relayed this story. It wasn't like my dad to be harsh. He was kind and affectionate and rarely displayed anger. But seeing the way my brother cried, there was no doubt that what had happened that day long ago had deeply wounded him. My brother then turned to my mother and confronted her for her response on that day: she had seemed like the ice queen. He was dying at the thought of her leaving, but she appeared cold and unfeeling. Not once had she even shed a tear. How could a mother send away her then-eight-year-old son for months at a time and not even cry at the thought of leaving him again? How could she stoically watch while her son's heart was being ravaged?

What my mother said next stunned me. Several times that day, she said she had cried, but she felt she had to be strong for my brother.

So whenever her emotions overwhelmed her, she ducked into a bathroom, cried for several minutes, regained her composure, and emerged as if nothing had happened. That day, she said, had ripped her apart. She hadn't wanted to leave my brother, but she felt she had no choice. All the missionaries sent their kids to boarding school (homeschooling wasn't commonly practiced) and to object was considered a sign of misplaced priorities, of placing your kids before God.

I was horrified by the perverse social pressure that had been placed on my parents, but I was also stunned by my mother's method of managing her emotions. I had never witnessed her retreat into a bathroom to cry or, before that day, heard her speak of it; but I knew her emotional management system well. In college I had done the same thing.

All four years of college, I struggled intensely with depression. I'm sure some of it stemmed from the usual coming-of-age identity issues. I had derived much of my childhood identity from my family name, but at school I was relatively anonymous. I also had been a stand-out athlete in high school, but in college I played only two lackluster seasons of women's basketball.

I also struggled spiritually. I attended a top evangelical school, so I had expected to find many deeply spiritual friends who loved Jesus. I'm sure those students existed, but I didn't find many of them. Most of the students I knew were well versed in spiritual lingo but seemed to lack any real passion for God. They also looked down on worship they deemed charismatic or emotionally expressive. But I was charismatic—not in the sense that I believed the gift of tongues was a litmus test for possessing the Holy Spirit, but I was very open to the Spirit and expressive in worship. The summer before coming to college, I had been mentored by some charismatic believers and introduced to a far more intimate relationship with Jesus than I had previously known was possible. But since this way of relating to God wasn't acceptable at my college, I buried my charismatic leanings. God soon felt increasingly distant, and I wondered if what I had experienced in high school was even real.

Through all of this, I maintained a happy exterior. As my mother had done so many years earlier, I'd duck into a bathroom—sometimes four or five times a day—to cry. I'd emerge fifteen to twenty minutes later as if nothing had ever happened. I was ashamed of being depressed. I felt I had a duty as a believer to be happy. I felt I had a duty as a member of my family to be independent and strong. I rarely called home, and I didn't let on. Until I opened up to the man who eventually became my husband, no one knew the depth of my struggle with depression.

Miraculously, God delivered me from my depression the summer after graduation. I'm reluctant to share the story because I know deliverance from depression usually isn't this easy. But for whatever reason, God lifted my depression in an instant. I was in the balcony of a Chicago-area megachurch, singing "Great Is Thy Faithfulness," when an overwhelming sense of God's love enveloped me. God, who had felt so far away for so long, seemed tangibly present. All my pent-up angst and loneliness surged to the surface, and I wept in the presence of the One I knew loved me and held me. After several minutes of basking in this presence, the depression was gone and I was changed.

So when I heard about my family's missionary experience, I felt deep empathy for my brother and for what he had endured. And I realized for the first time that I had obtained my dysfunctional way of managing my emotions from my mother. But since my parents had returned to the States before I had reached school age and I had never gone to boarding school, I assumed I had emerged from our family's missionary experience otherwise unscathed.

I was wrong.

Though I didn't realize it until years later, the trauma of sending my brother and also my oldest sister to boarding school had severely impacted my mother's ability to connect emotionally with her kids. This created a deficit in me that later threatened to shipwreck my life.

BROKEN

One hot, humid night I was in bed, struggling to sleep. I kicked the covers off my legs to find some relief. The fan whirled above my head, making an annoying click with every revolution. I rolled from the fetal position onto my back and sighed. I was too hot to sleep, but too tired to get up. Something was bothering me, but I couldn't put my finger on what it was. Then I rolled toward the inside of the bed and gasped. There, lying between my husband and me, was Sarah.[1] I snapped to a sitting position, blinked, and looked at the bed again. Sarah was gone. It was just a dream. But I was shaken.

I'm not normally someone who analyzes my dreams, but occasionally I have dreams that I know are significant. Whether it was my heart symbolically projecting something through my subconscious or God speaking directly through a dream, I didn't know. But wide-eyed and heart pounding, I recognized it as a warning. My relationship with Sarah had become obsessive.

Everything had begun innocuously enough. Sarah was a troubled teen whose tumultuous home life drove her to self-destructive behaviors, and as her youth leader, I tried to help her. But my need to rescue her was sabotaging my marriage. Helping her consumed almost all my emotional energy, and the intensity of our relationship left little room for Neal. My dream shocked me into facing this reality, but I was so emotionally entangled that I had no idea how to extricate myself. How on earth did this happen? I was in my midthirties, had been married nearly fifteen years, and had two boys in elementary school. How did I get entangled in an emotionally dysfunctional relationship with a former student in our church youth group? What did it mean? How could I ever get my normal life back?

I was confused and distraught. At the time I didn't know what codependency was, but I was deeply embroiled in it. I'd stay up half the night wondering if Sarah was okay. Then, when she'd cut off communication, as she often did, I'd pursue her aggressively. The more I'd pursue, the more she'd run, and the more I'd pursue. I became so preoccupied with rescuing Sarah from her endless dramas that my marriage suffered. My children suffered. My relationship with Jesus suffered. But I was determined. I was doing God's work. I was saving a lost soul. I was, in truth, so messed up that I couldn't see straight.

My husband and I were going to marriage counseling at the time. Youth ministry had taken its toll on us, and the line between our ministry and personal lives had become blurred, even nonexistent. I had told our counselor about my childhood habit of rescuing stray animals. The more desperate and pathetic they were, the more I wanted to shelter and care for them. So when I described Sarah to my counselor, she exclaimed, "So, you've just gone from saving stray animals to saving stray people!" I knew she was right and that this insight was significant. I just didn't know how or why.

Sarah was one of the most gifted and charismatic people I have ever known, but in some ways she was a stray—lost and looking for a home. She had two parents living in her home, but both of them were so broken themselves that they were unable to provide the emotional support and boundaries she needed.

I first met Sarah when she was a senior in high school. A friend brought her to our youth ministry, and I immediately liked her. Over time I got to know her well, and she began to open up about her family. Her father was an alcoholic, a truly pitiable person if there ever was one. He was kind and generous but haunted by his past. Sarah told me that he had been abused by his own brothers as a boy and was constantly trying to drown his demons with alcohol. But he'd had a radical conversion experience when Sarah and her sister were little girls. He had sobered up, had begun taking the family to church, and for several years had been the father Sarah and her sister had always wanted. But then something snapped and he returned to the bottle, began avoiding friends from church, and retreated into himself. By the time Sarah and I met, he was completely absent. He never came to any of her events, and when he was home, he was never truly present. A few years after my relationship with Sarah ended, he committed suicide.

Had Sarah's mother been emotionally available to her, her father's devolution might have been bearable. But her mother, who apparently possessed much of Sarah's charm and charisma, used her skills to manipulate her daughter to satisfy her own narcissistic needs. I remember two of Sarah's friends once recounting that they saw her mother speak kindly and affectionately to Sarah one minute. Then, without any seeming provocation, she started screaming and belittling Sarah. Sarah hated her mother, but she desperately loved and needed her too. Whenever Sarah talked about her, I could see the tangled web of love, hate, and need fighting a tug-of-war inside her.

I felt immense compassion for Sarah and communicated it. Given her incredible need for love and attention, she soaked it in—and she took note that I had a need, too, one I'm convinced she was aware of long before I was. She had her mother's keen emotional perception, and her ability to manipulate. For reasons neither of us knew at the time, I needed to be needed by Sarah and to take care of her. Just as I had with those stray dogs and cats, I felt a compulsion to rescue

Sarah. Sarah would exploit this need, often relaying stories of horrific things her mother had done to her and making her appear to be in need of saving. She'd also relate things that her mother would say about me, indicating how jealous her mother was of the relationship I shared with her daughter. I'd seemingly brush these things off, but deep down I liked taking her mother's place. I liked being needed and playing the role of savior.

Sarah also had a pattern of drawing close and then suddenly retreating like a scared and wounded animal. One day she would divulge some deep, dark secret to me, then for two weeks she would refuse my calls, miss our appointments, and ignore my e-mails. Given the nature of what she had just shared, I'd assume she was so fragile and wounded that she couldn't face me. So I'd shift into pursuit mode, calling and texting and trying to prove to her that I wasn't like all those awful people who had hurt her. I realize now that she was simply manipulating me to fill the gaping hole in her soul.

Complicating matters was the fact that Sarah had begun singing in a band I was leading. I had never really aspired to be a musician, but shortly before meeting Sarah, I had started writing worship songs for my congregation. At a friend's urging, I formed a band and started recording my songs. I really wanted Sarah to record them with me. She had a captivating voice—folksy and rich, like a mix between Joni Mitchell and Tracy Chapman. Sarah also could create entrancing harmonies and convey the emotion of a song like no one I had ever known. I loved the blend of our voices, and singing together became like a drug to me.

Eventually Sarah divulged that she struggled with attraction to other women. She also told me about a relationship she had with a lesbian that she feared might become romantic. As a professing believer who had grown up in the church, she knew that the Bible condemned same-sex relationships and said she didn't want to go there. I didn't know much about same-sex attraction at the time, but given Sarah's immense wounding from her father and especially her mother, I wasn't surprised.

My determination to rescue Sarah intensified. I had friends who were part of a healing ministry that helped people with all sorts of troubles, including sexual brokenness, so I talked to them about how to help Sarah. Soon they sensed that Sarah wasn't the only person who needed help. "I'm not sure you're the one to help Sarah," a leader told me. "You seem too emotionally invested in this." I was furious. They didn't know me—or Sarah. How dare they! "I think maybe you should let go of the relationship and let someone else step in," the leader urged. I shrugged off her suggestion and decided I was going to save Sarah. I was uniquely positioned to help her. She needed me.

The truth is I couldn't let go. I didn't want to give up singing with Sarah; I couldn't imagine someone else taking her place. Beyond that, I didn't want to give up the relationship. I had become emotionally hooked, and the thought of ending the relationship killed me. Deep down I knew something was seriously wrong, but I didn't want to admit it. I couldn't admit it. That is, until I had the dream. I didn't know what to call what I was experiencing. I didn't know how or why I had gotten so emotionally entangled with someone so incredibly dysfunctional and needy. But I knew our relationship was unhealthy and dangerous. I needed to get help.

JOURNEY OF DISCOVERY

This began a journey of discovery—into my past, into the reality of my brokenness, into reliance on Jesus like never before—that eventually led to recovery and healing. I didn't have to end my relationship with Sarah; she did it for me, running off with the woman she had told me about and cutting off all communication. I was wrecked. My relationship with Sarah had opened up an incredible need and longing inside me while simultaneously satiating it. I felt as if I were going through withdrawal. It was excruciatingly painful, but the death of my relationship with Sarah was a severe mercy. God had lovingly if brutally opened up this wounded place in my soul, and He was going to perform surgery.

Best-selling authors and counselors Frank Minirth, Paul Meier, and Robert Hemfelt say codependents are like "a vacuum cleaner gone wild," constantly drawing others into their dysfunctional world as they "struggle relentlessly to fill the great emotional vacuum within themselves."[2] Obviously I had my own void that had made me susceptible, but Sarah was like a vacuum cleaner, and I was like a piece of lint—unsuspecting, powerless, and consumed.

I wasn't the only straight person who ever got sucked into her emotional vortex, and I thank God my relationship with Sarah never developed into anything physical. To this day I'm not even sure how to describe that relationship. But the experience made me suspect that all the categories of attraction our culture has so skillfully created aren't nearly as cut-and-dried as everyone thinks. Maybe we all live and relate along a spectrum of health and dysfunction, and left unchecked and unguarded, our hearts and certain circumstances can combine to lead us into places we never imagined possible.

I was afraid of how my husband would respond when I admitted to him the depth of my emotional dependency on Sarah. I felt unbearable shame. I felt broken, needy, and defective. But Neal didn't see me that way at all. I'll never forget the night I confessed my dream to him. I broke down crying several times just trying to explain to him what was going on inside of me. When I finally did, he looked at me with eyes rich in compassion and love and promised me we'd get through it. By God's grace, we did. And my friends' healing ministry that I had envisioned Sarah joining became the venue God used to heal me.

What I discovered over the next twelve to eighteen months was that I had grown up with a deficit—and that deficit had deeply affected me. My mother, someone I deeply loved and admired, was largely cut off from me emotionally. As a child I had hugged and cuddled my dad more than I had my mom. Yet I considered my mother and me to be quite close. When I was in high school, for example, I would come home from school every day and sit up on the kitchen counter. While she'd cook dinner, I'd share everything that had happened that day. Even as an adult, when we'd visit my parents, my mom and I would talk for hours and hours about a myriad of topics. We especially enjoyed discussing spiritual things. My mother was one of the wisest and most spiritual people I knew, and together we would plumb the depths of theology, ministry, and the nature of God. I loved my mother and thoroughly enjoyed being with her, but we rarely discussed personal things. When I was in high school, she sometimes didn't even know whom I was dating. I wouldn't tell my mother about personal struggles either. I always got the sense that these things would seem trivial to her, so I didn't mention them.

My mother never shared her emotions with me either. Even when she got cancer and her hair fell out during chemotherapy, she never expressed weakness. My mother was a rock. She never complained. She never worried. She hardly ever cried. In many ways I was in awe of her and still am, though she's long since passed away. She was my hero—strong, competent, smart—yet emotionally inaccessible.

My mother is no longer around to explain why she parented as she did, but I think I understand. No mother should have to send her child away at age eight. It would have destroyed me to do that, but my mother had to do it twice, with my brother and my oldest sister, and she felt she couldn't share her true feelings about having to do so. She sucked it up, pretended to be happy, and moved on. So by the time I came along, she had detached emotionally from her kids for her own protection. In essence, she killed her emotions. It's a testament to her that she pulled it off as well as she did.

Each of us kids was affected by this detachment in different ways and to different degrees. It produced in me an unmet need for intimacy and attachment that remained largely buried until Sarah unearthed it. I was an extremely sensitive child who probably craved emotional intimacy and physical touch more than most. When I didn't receive that from my mother, I learned to cope. I did what my mother had modeled for me. I sucked it up. I moved on and didn't give it much thought. But occasionally something would awaken this unmet need. I attended summer camp as a preteen girl and remember basking in the motherly attention of my counselor. I'm sure many girls do that, but looking back I realize I craved that attention more than most.

Sarah evoked that longing in a way no one else had ever done before. Psychologists call what I did *projective identification*. The concept is Freudian, which makes me uncomfortable with it since I don't buy into the theory that our unconscious minds, with all their primitive needs and impulses, govern our adult behaviors. That said, I do believe Freud recognized and studied a real human phenomenon that can control us if we let it. Essentially what I did was project part of myself onto Sarah. She was me—but not the strong and competent me I presented to everyone else. She was the wounded me I kept hidden inside, the daughter craving connection with a mom who remained largely unreachable. Sarah's wounding was far more severe than mine, but seeing Sarah's agony opened up mine. And in some confused and messed-up way, by soothing Sarah I was nurturing myself. I'm sure that's also why I collected stray animals. By nurturing them I was nurturing myself.

As an adult I couldn't go back and get something from my mother I had failed to get as a child, yet I was left with this intense need and unmet longing—and the temptation to anesthetize it all. I knew no human being or drug was capable of healing me, and after the horrific emotional roller coaster with Sarah, I had no desire to get on another one. I recognized my only hope was Jesus. Only by supernatural intervention could I ever regain some semblance of health and normalcy. I felt broken and helpless, but by God's grace I maintained a mustard seed of faith and hope. Jesus had healed me of depression years earlier, and I had faith that He would heal me of this. I suspected that this healing would not be instantaneous; it would be slow and grueling. I knew Jesus would not abandon me because in His Word He promised to transform me, and I clung to that promise with everything I had.

UNIQUELY FEMININE?

In their best-selling book, *Love Is a Choice*, Drs. Minirth, Meier, and Hemfelt estimate that at least one in four Americans struggles with codependency. By their calculations, codependency is "an epidemic of staggering degree," affecting at least one hundred million Americans.[3] Though no universally accepted definition of codependency exists, the bulk of codependency literature seems to agree on several core characteristics of the disorder. These include an "excessive reliance on other people for approval and identity"; "the tendency to put other people's needs ahead of one's own"; and "the tendency to engage in interpersonal behaviors such as 'caretaking' (taking responsibility for regulating another person's behavior) and 'rescuing' (fixing up the damage caused by another person's irresponsible behavior)."[4] As one licensed counselor put it, codependency is "an addiction to another person; the compulsive need to control that part of their life that is out-of-control."[5]

Before my relationship with Sarah, I never would have imagined that I would be susceptible to codependency. Normally in mentoring relationships I maintained appropriate boundaries and never did for someone else what she should do for herself. On one level I understood how I had become codependent: my life circumstances had created the conditions for a perfect storm of dysfunction, and Sarah was the ideal candidate to unleash it. Still, I was surprised that I had behaved so unlike my usual self.

Strangely though, this affirmed my feminine identity. Until this point in my life, I had never felt as if I belonged to my gender in a unique way. I was equally if not more comfortable in a man's world than in a woman's world. I felt at home in the newsroom, for example, but at women's events at church I often felt like a fish out of water, especially when asked to create crafts, which I rarely enjoyed. I also found that when men and women would talk about their differences, I could relate equally to the stereotypical characteristics of both sexes. Christian marriage events were the worst. They would always talk about how men wanted respect and women wanted to be cherished. Yes, I wanted to be cherished, but growing up as the youngest in a family that valued achievement, I definitely wanted respect too. So I never felt particularly feminine or womanly, no matter how it was defined.

By succumbing to codependency, though, I was actually displaying something predominantly female. Men rarely fall prey to codependency. Peter Vegso, president of a publishing company that specializes in self-help books, once asserted that 85 percent of the codependency market is female.[6] Feminists attribute women's increased susceptibility to cultural factors, saying it is merely the result of being conditioned to function as nurturers and caretakers. Others say our susceptibility stems from our inborn nature: we are wired for relationships and have an increased ability and need to bond and to empathize.[7]

I knew I hadn't been conditioned to be codependent. I was conditioned to be fiercely independent, and had I been a man, I probably could have pulled it off. I'd be the island—strong and resilient and needing no one.[8] But almost despite myself, I possessed a feminine soul. No matter how hard I tried, I couldn't exist without close emotional connection—to God, as my bout with depression had showed, and to people, as my struggle with codependency had made clear. It's as though I had been hardwired for close relationship, and when I didn't get it, I resorted to a uniquely female way of coping.

I wasn't sure what all this meant, but my egalitarian worldview had been dealt a serious blow. *Perhaps men and women are not essentially the same*, I thought, *but fundamentally different—not just in their anatomy, but in the very deepest parts of their being. And if that's true, might some of my other egalitarian assumptions be false?* I wasn't sure, but I was open and hungry for answers. And I was teachable. God had used the experience to break and humble me, and now I was ready to receive.

THREE

SEX, SEXISM, AND SACRAMENT

For Anna Duggar, the revelations about her husband, Josh, must have come as a complete shock. Josh had first captured Anna's heart at the age of sixteen by espousing a commitment to God and purity when he appeared in the Duggar family's first reality TV special called, *14 Children and Pregnant Again!* "As my family watched the video," Anna wrote on her and Josh's website, "I noticed how Joshua, then age sixteen, shared the importance of guarding his heart and waiting for someone who would really love him and wasn't going to just get carried away with their emotions. I was so excited to see another family who was brought up so similar to the way our parents were training us, but never would I have dreamed what God had in store!"[1]

Anna's statement now seems cruelly ironic. The idyllic home she believed she and Josh were sharing was revealed in 2015 to be a facade. That's when Josh disclosed that, as a teenager, he had molested five girls, including some of his sisters. Just three months later, he further stunned fans by confessing he had cheated on his wife and harbored an Internet porn addiction.[2] Then came allegations that Josh had twice sexually assaulted porn star Danica Dillon[3] and signed up for two paid subscriptions to Ashley Madison, a website that facilitates extramarital affairs.[4]

For a woman such as Anna, who believed wholeheartedly in the goodness of her spouse, these revelations must have been devastating. Given the circumstances, one would expect Anna's Christian community to rally to her support. Stunningly, though, some appeared to blame Anna for Josh's infidelity, implying that she was at fault for not adequately satisfying her husband. Soon after Josh admitted to his affairs, the Duggars' family pastor said in a sermon on infidelity, "If a husband or wife fails to keep his or her partner happy sexually, they are opening themselves up to the attack of the enemy. . . . And that enemy is going to take your spouse away from you."[5]

Anna Duggar's mother-in-law, Michelle Duggar, wrote something similar in an article posted to her blog soon after Josh's confession. The mother of nineteen wrote that wives should always be available to meet their husbands' sexual needs, even when they are exhausted or pregnant. "He can get his lunch somewhere else," Duggar wrote. "But you are the only one who can meet that special need that he has in his life for intimacy. . . . So be available, and not just available, but be joyfully available for him. Smile and be willing to say, 'Yes, sweetie, I am here for you,' no matter what."[6]

Normally I ignore dramas involving reality TV stars. I'm not a fan of the genre and have never actually seen an episode of the former TLC program *19 Kids and Counting*. But when I read reports that Anna Duggar was being blamed for Josh's infidelity, I was disgusted—so much so that I wrote an article rebutting the accusation for *Her.meneutics*, *Christianity Today*'s former online blog for women.[7] Essentially I argued that each person is responsible for his or her own sins and that adultery comes from a greedy, lustful heart, not an insufficient wife. The article clearly struck a chord, receiving more than seventy-five hundred Facebook shares and more than one hundred comments.

Most agreed with my premise. However, several readers, mostly men, objected, citing 1 Corinthians 7:5, which says, "Do not deprive each other except perhaps by mutual consent and for a time, so that you may devote yourselves to prayer. Then come together again so that Satan will not tempt you because of your lack of self-control" (NIV). One wrote, "The Bible teaches us not to withhold sex from our spouses because that brings temptation. . . . The author of this article writes: 'This (because lust is insatiable) is why wives simply offering sex as frequently as their husbands request it does not ensure fidelity. In fact, this practice may exacerbate the lust problem.' But this is contrary to 1 Corinthians. She is encouraging women to deny their husbands and this is wrong."

Another reader wrote, "It seems like there is a harsh warning (in Scripture) against causing someone to stumble. I wonder if this applies in this situation. Maybe someone drove their husband or wife crazy with their sin (of commission or omission) and do have *some* culpability in their choice. . . . 1 Cor. 7: 5 seems to support that. Can one spouse cause the other to stumble? It seems to me like they are one of the most likely people to have influence on their spouse's behavior."

These comments, and the attitude they represented, made me sick to my stomach. I recognize that a marriage's health, or lack of it, can influence a person's decision to commit adultery. Certainly sexual intimacy in marriage is important, and frequency of sex can be a barometer of a marriage's health. But these men seemed willing and even eager to twist 1 Corinthians 7:5 into an unconditional command to have sex. That some men would treat their wives in this manner was revolting, as were the view of women as mere sex objects and the view of marriage as a one-sided service arrangement in which men selfishly use their wives for their own gratification.

Unfortunately, this perverse view of sex and marriage is widespread in the patriarchy movement, an extreme form of complementarianism[8] to which the Duggars subscribe. All complementarians affirm male leadership in the church and home, but patriarchy codifies male authority into a rigid set of rules that goes beyond traditional interpretations of Scripture. Adherents teach that a daughter, even as a grown adult, must remain under her father's authority until she is married; that a woman should not be allowed to vote, unless of course she's duplicating her husband's vote; and that higher education is unimportant for women.[9] After all, who needs a mind when your husband can do all the thinking for you? The movement is rife with misogynistic attitudes and transforms marriage into a benevolent dictatorship at best or, as in the case of Josh Duggar, a malevolent one.

Not surprisingly, some prominent Christian leaders, including those who identify as complementarians, have publicly distanced themselves from the patriarchy movement. Michael Farris, founder of the Homeschool Legal Defense Association and Patrick Henry College, wrote a stinging indictment of the patriarchy movement in 2014, claiming that it damages people and misrepresents Scripture. "In sum, patriarchy teaches that women in general should be subject to men in general," Farris wrote. "The Bible teaches no such thing."[10]

What does the Bible really teach about men and women? And what is the true purpose of sex and marriage? As I wrestled with these questions in my twenties and early thirties, I couldn't find satisfactory answers in either the complementarian or the egalitarian camp. I wasn't aware of the patriarchy movement at the time, but the inordinate focus on sex roles in complementarian churches I attended evoked a similar emotional response in me as the Duggar scandal had. To me, the driving force behind complementarianism seemed to be a desire for men to control women. I had no sense of any larger picture, nor was I given any compelling vision that captured my imagination. Complementarianism just seemed like a set of oppressive rules, which I decided I would rather avoid.

During the season of healing that followed my dysfunctional relationship with Sarah, I also began to notice serious flaws with the egalitarian vision. To say that men and women were equal in function seemed to imply that sex was merely a biological trait, and that in every other way human beings were neuters. However, the healing course I took taught the exact opposite. It taught that our maleness and femaleness extends deep into our souls and is bound up in symbol. A woman with a compassionate and loving mother, for example, is likely to symbolize the feminine in her heart in a very positive way, and as a result embrace and embody femininity in a healthy and integrated fashion. But a woman with a cold, manipulative, or passive mother may have a distorted symbol of the feminine, and as a result reject part of herself and suffer from any number of emotional, sexual, and/or psychological problems. Interestingly, the program I was in never addressed people's feelings directly. Instead, it focused on correcting broken symbols in people's hearts. As a result, proper feelings seemed to emerge naturally.

This deep and symbolic way of thinking about gender and sexuality was entirely new to me. As an evangelical, I didn't really value symbols. I was suspicious of them. After all, evangelicalism is in large part a reaction to empty and rote religion, which—ironically—is what symbols (at least religious ones) symbolize to evangelicals. Yet the program helped me realize we are all symbolic creatures and our minds and hearts are constantly attaching intangible concepts to tangible things. Depending on our experiences, these symbols may have different meanings and evoke different feelings in different people. This understanding set the stage for me to understand why God had created male and female and why He had instituted marriage. But for years, I couldn't put all the pieces together into a comprehensive vision. Complementarian marriage continued to symbolize male domination to me, and egalitarian marriage symbolized freedom. So despite the problems I recognized with egalitarianism, I still clung to it, though half-heartedly.

What I didn't realize at the time was that I was longing for an overarching symbol that would give me an inspiring vision of marriage and would make sense of these profound differences between men and women. I longed for something that showed how husband and wife could work together for their mutual benefit, not just the benefit of one sex, and something that called us together for a purpose greater than ourselves. That beautiful and transcendent symbol was right there in the pages of Scripture, but for years I couldn't see it.

SEARCHING FOR MEANING

I have always suspected that gender, sexuality, and sex roles pointed to something greater than was taught in church. Growing up I heard that sex roles were there to establish order. The husband had to be the head of the home or there would be anarchy. Without headship, who would make a decision in the case of an impasse? And sex was sort of a necessary evil. Christian leaders would talk (nervously) about sex being good and a gift from God, but the majority of the references to sex were negative. The all-important message was to just say no! That is, until you were married.

Perhaps in reaction to this prudish presentation, evangelicals in the seventies and eighties began to tip the scales in the other direction and emphasize the sensual joys of married sex. My husband and I encountered this new direction when we were in premarital counseling and our counselor recommended we read *Intended for Pleasure*, by Ed and Gaye Wheat. The book was essentially a sex manual filled with diagrams and techniques designed to help couples "develop a thrilling, happy marriage."[11] The book repulsed me. Yes, I was looking forward to having a satisfying sexual relationship with my husband, but not because we would master the mechanics of sex. I had hoped sex would be about expressing love and about an emotional, maybe even spiritual, connection.

Dr. Wheat's book did contain a hint that sex might have some deeper dimension. It referenced Ephesians 5:31–32 (KJV), which says that the one-flesh union of a husband and wife reveals a "great mystery" concerning Christ and the church. But to Dr. Wheat, this great mystery was merely that "the properly and lovingly executed and mutually satisfying sexual union" shows us how Jesus Christ "is intimately involved with and loves the church."[12] Dr. Wheat never really explained how well-performed sex reflects God's love for the church. And honestly, the concept seemed so foreign that I essentially discarded it for the next fifteen years.

The same could probably be said about male headship in our home. Clearly, the concept was in Scripture, but I really didn't have any idea what that actually meant. Plus, I had a strong natural aversion to one-way submission. Whenever that topic came up, I'd point to the need for mutual submission in marriage, but I didn't really have a positive picture of what that looked like either. So in many ways our marriage operated on autopilot. I did what came naturally, which, given that I came from a relatively healthy family, often worked. But it sometimes didn't work. To be quite honest, in the early years, I muddled through marriage and motherhood much as I muddled through serving in a male-dominated church. I tried the best I could to honor God in these areas of my life, but I didn't have a clear picture of God's design or what God intended for marriage. That is, until my late thirties, when some close friends introduced us to something called *The Theology of the Body* (TOB).

The Theology of the Body is a study of what God has revealed about Himself in and through the human body, based on dozens of sermons by Pope John Paul II. As an evangelical, my first reaction to this teaching was skepticism. It came from a pope, and like most evangelicals I had a pretty dim view of Catholicism, believing that the Catholic Church was rife with corruption and taught a works-based salvation. However, my view of Catholicism had been softening over the years as I encountered more and more Catholics who exhibited truly vibrant faith. I also had long admired the Catholic Church for upholding the sanctity of life when many evangelicals were rationalizing abortion, so I was open to what John Paul II had to say. Perhaps most convincing were my friends, whom I greatly respected and who were Wheaton College graduates like my husband and me. They were so enthusiastic about John Paul's TOB that I figured it must have merit. So I began reading articles and books by Christopher West, a world-renowned expert and popularizer of TOB.

As I explored John Paul's Theology of the Body, I realized it convincingly answered the fundamental questions concerning gender and sexuality that no one else seemed able to answer. It explained why God created male and female, as well as human sexuality, beyond the obvious pragmatic reasons. It suggested why the functions of men and women must be different; however, it presented a vision of gendered complementarity that was beautiful and compelling rather than demeaning and oppressive.

TOB'S SACRAMENTAL VIEW OF
THE BODY AND SEXUALITY

John Paul II's TOB is based on the notion that the human body is a sacrament, though he does not mean that the body is equal to the sacraments of the church, such as baptism and communion. The body is a sacrament in the broader sense. It is a symbol revealing a mystery of God.[13] This is consistent with Genesis 1:26–27, which teaches that God made man in *imago Dei*—God's image. Most Protestants equate this *imago Dei* with nonmaterial qualities, such as the human will or soul, but John Paul asserted that God's image is also reflected in our physical bodies. As Richard M. Hogan and John M. LeVoir state in *Covenant of Love*, paraphrasing John Paul, the body is "a physical image of God, an outward sign of how God acts. We are not just images of God in our interior structure, in the powers of thinking and choosing, but also physically in the body."[14] Or, as John Paul said in a 1980 sermon, "The body, and it alone, is capable of making visible what is invisible: the spiritual and the divine. It was created to transfer into the visible reality of the world the mystery hidden since time immemorial in God, and thus be a sign of it."[15]

Specifically John Paul taught that our bodies reveal two mysteries of God. First, our bodies (specifically our sexuality) reveal the mystery of God's Trinitarian love. The Trinity is probably one of the most mind-blowing concepts in all of Christianity. How can God be one yet exist eternally as three distinct Persons—Father, Son, and Holy Spirit? John Paul taught that God stamped this theology right on our bodies. Clearly the male body is not made to exist in solitude but to be united with the female body, which complements it. Likewise the female body is made to be united to the male body, which complements it. When we read in Genesis 2:24 that Adam and Eve—the twin bearers of God's image—became "one flesh," God is giving us a beautiful symbol of Himself. He is demonstrating how distinct persons can become one. In doing so, He's revealing the profound mystery of Trinitarian life and love.

When I first heard this concept, I actually cried. The idea that human sexuality reflected the mystery of God's Trinitarian love resonated strongly inside me. This concept made the marital union something far deeper, more profound, and much nobler than anything I would have ever imagined. And it presented a compelling vision of marriage that was thoroughly complementarian, yet void of any male domination or human selfishness. This vision didn't provide a list of dos and don'ts; it filled my imagination with something good and beautiful and invited me to live in this glorious reality.

The reality of Trinitarian life and love is not the only mystery revealed by the marital union. In Ephesians 5, the apostle Paul refers to the one-flesh union of husband and wife as "a profound mystery" revealing "Christ and the church" (v. 32 NIV). I must have read that passage dozens of times, but it never really struck me what it meant. Reading TOB, it finally clicked: the sexual union of husband and wife is also a symbol of Christ's union with His church. I'll admit, something about that seemed scandalous to me. Did God really intend for me to think of sex with my husband as analogous to union with Christ? That's precisely what John Paul (and the apostle Paul) taught: "In this entire world, there is not a more perfect, more complete image of God, Unity and Community. There is no other human reality which corresponds more, humanly speaking, to that divine mystery."[16]

This cast sex and marriage in an entirely new light for me, although I realized this was not a novel idea. I remembered learning in my college Bible classes that throughout the Old Testament, God refers to His relationship with His people, the Israelites, as a husband-wife relationship. In Hosea 2:20, for example, the prophet says to Israel, "And you shall know the LORD." And here, Hosea uses the same Hebrew word for *know* that is used in Genesis 4:1, where "Adam knew Eve his wife, and she conceived and bore Cain."

In the New Testament this spousal imagery continues. In Ephesians 5:25, Paul encourages husbands to love their wives as Christ does the church. In 2 Corinthians 11:2, Paul, speaking of the church, says, "I promised you to one husband, to Christ, so that I might present you as a pure virgin to him" (NIV). And in Revelation 19:9, the church is presented to Christ as a bride to a bridegroom at the "marriage supper of the Lamb." John Paul argued in TOB that marriage is the great metaphor of Scripture: the Bible begins with the marriage of Adam and Eve and ends with the wedding of Christ and His church. These, John Paul says, are the nuptial "bookends" of Scripture, and should be used as a "key for interpreting what lies between." Popular Catholic theologian Christopher West wrote, "From this analogical perspective we come to understand that God's mysterious and eternal plan is to espouse us to himself forever . . . to 'marry' us."[17]

I had heard these kinds of statements before, but I had never quite grasped them. Now I got it—and it touched me deeply. Gender, marriage, sexuality—it was all designed to help us understand God and how He relates to us. God desires a relationship with us that is so personal, so intimate, and so completely unified that He created two genders and human sexuality to express it. This was a staggering thought and revolutionized my entire understanding of sex, marriage, family—and gender roles. Before encountering TOB I never would have thought that I could become complementarian, but TOB erased all the objections I had to complementarianism. I realized that embracing a true biblical vision of gendered difference didn't mean succumbing to male domination or denying women's gifts. It meant living into a whole new reality where men and women functioned in concert, rather than competition, and together reflected the glory of God. The vision communicated in TOB gave me a blueprint for marriage and ministry that worked and helped both sexes to flourish.

TOB AND SEX ROLES IN MARRIAGE

John Paul's sacramental teaching about the body, marriage, and sexuality elevated my understanding of symbol to a whole new level. I saw that the relational truths of Christianity are not contained merely in a series of propositions. They are also embodied in a symbolic system designed to help us understand awesome, transcendent realities. Leanne Payne, a pioneer in healing ministry whose writings figured prominently in the healing course I took, once wrote, "Reality is simply far too great to be contained in propositions. That is why man needs gestures, pictures, images, rhythms, metaphor, symbol, and myth."[18] Or, as Christian thinker and writer Alan Jones said, "Symbols bind up reality for us. When the symbols die, we die too."[19]

I am convinced that one of the reasons the church is so vulnerable to attacks against orthodoxy is that we have forsaken symbols. One cannot understand gender and sexuality without also understanding the importance of symbol. And without a proper understanding of gender and sexuality, we cannot understand God or how we relate to Him.

Increasingly Protestants are awakening to the symbolic significance of sexuality and marriage. In his book *The Meaning of Sex*, Dennis Hollinger, president and professor of Christian ethics at Gordon-Conwell Theological Seminary, acknowledged marriage as an icon of the Trinity: "In sex a couple reflects something of the very image of God, for it points to a oneness of two which mirrors the oneness of the Triune Godhead."[20] Similarly Russell Moore, president of the Religious Liberty Commission of the Southern Baptist Convention, spoke eloquently about the symbolic meaning of marriage and family when he addressed a worldwide gathering of religious leaders at the Vatican in 2014. "The family structure is not an arbitrary expression of nature or of the will of God," he said. "Marriage and family are instead archetypes, icons of God's purpose for the universe."[21]

Understanding our symbolic roles as men and women is critical for understanding God and His purposes. It's also crucial for understanding sex roles. When we know the primary reason for gender and sexuality is symbolic, then we realize that sex roles are not ultimately important; the symbols and what they reflect are ultimately important. Sex roles are merely a means of preserving the integrity of these extremely important symbols. They are a way to ensure that we, as men and women, act in a way that is congruent with the spiritual reality God has ordained for us to reflect.

This was a major epiphany for me. Finally I realized why God had established specific roles for men and women. He was not acting arbitrarily or preferentially but instead protecting our symbolic functions of proclaiming the mystery of the Godhead and Christ's relationship to His church. In some ways this diminished the importance of sex roles. They are not an end in themselves, but merely a means to an end. In other ways this elevated the importance of sex roles because what they help preserve is so vital. It also elevated the importance of marriage and family. If our marriages are God's way of communicating to the world His triune love and Christ's relationship with the church, then the stakes for our marriages are high.

As I reflected on this profound reality, it dawned on me that complementarians have it both right and wrong. They are right that men and women have different functions. After all, the roles within the

Trinity are not interchangeable. Though equal and sharing the same divine nature, each Person of the Godhead has a specific function. For example, God the Father sends the Son[22] and the Holy Spirit,[23] not vice versa. Jesus has a special role as the Savior of the world, becoming incarnate as a man and paying for sins by dying on the cross.[24] The Holy Spirit fills believers and acts as a counselor, guiding and convicting us of sins and helping us live holy lives.[25] Similarly, the roles of Christ and His church are not interchangeable. Christ sacrifices Himself for the church, and the church responds by receiving His sacrifice and then following His leadership. If these are our twin models for marriage, then it follows that the roles of husbands and wives are not interchangeable.

A sacramental understanding of gender and sexuality also suggests there is hierarchy in marriage, as complementarians hold, because there is hierarchy in the Godhead. Jesus, for example, clearly submitted to the Father. According to Philippians 2:6–8, Jesus "did not count equality with God a thing to be grasped, but emptied himself, by taking the form of a servant." Similarly, in John 6:38, Jesus says that He came from heaven not to do His will, "but to do the will of him who sent me" (NIV). The Spirit likewise testifies not about Himself but about Jesus.[26]

However, complementarians err when they focus so much on the proper execution of roles that this eclipses, and sometimes completely obscures, the intended purpose of sex roles. This is how complementarians, even at their best, miss the forest for the trees: they teach husbands and wives how to play their appropriate roles, but they fail to cast a vision for the grander purpose of marriage. As a result, men often use their positions to gain control or advantage, completely perverting the reality marriage is supposed to symbolize. And women either submit to this abuse and lose a proper sense of self, or become angry and reactive, turning their marriages into battlegrounds. But in the Godhead, exploitation is unthinkable; there is only trust, mutuality, and love. The

Father, though He has the position of supreme authority, takes delight in glorifying the Son,[27] just as the Son delights in glorifying the Father, and the Spirit delights in glorifying both the Father and the Son. This is the transcendent reality our marriages are meant to reflect.

The apostle Paul taught that marital hierarchy should never be self-seeking. Instead, mirroring the love of God, it should protect, trust, hope, and persevere.[28] Giving a gender-specific charge to husbands, he tells them, "Love your wives, as Christ loved the church and gave himself up for her." Then, drawing equally on the analogy of Christ and the church, and the oneness of the Trinity, Paul says, "Husbands should love their wives as their own bodies. He who loves his wife loves himself. For no one ever hated his own flesh, but nourishes and cherishes it, just as Christ does the church, because we are members of his body."[29] As Russell Moore notes, "The relationship between a husband and wife is not that of a business model or a corporate organizational chart but is instead an organic unity."[30] It is a reflection of God's love.

TOB FOR SINGLES

Because TOB has such direct application to marriage, it's easy for singles to feel left out. But John Paul, a man committed to lifelong celibacy, didn't feel that way at all. He considered celibacy a more immediate participation in the eternal union of Christ and his bride, the church. By forsaking marriage for the kingdom of God, John Paul believed he was skipping the symbol of the mystical marriage with Christ for an anticipation of the actual marriage itself. In celibacy, he was choosing to embrace the ache of solitude that Adam felt in the garden, yet rather than satisfying that longing for communion with another person, he chose instead to direct his longing directly to God.[31]

This anticipation of marriage to Christ is strikingly portrayed in a nun's initiation into a convent. I will never forget the first time I witnessed this ceremony. It was portrayed in an old movie and I found it profoundly moving. The young woman being initiated wore a white wedding dress. Then, in an actual wedding ceremony, she was symbolically married to Christ and pledged to him for life. As I watched this ceremony, it awakened in me a longing to do the same. In some ways, I felt jealous of the nun who could devote herself to Jesus in such an immediate and undivided way. And I understood, perhaps for the very first time, why the apostle Paul said "it is good for (the unmarried and widows) to stay unmarried as I do."[32]

Of course, many singles are single out of necessity, not choice. Still, when singles remain chaste because of their devotion to the Lord, they are doing so for the kingdom. And like a nun or priest, they can use their solitary experience to drive them closer to God. They also can still embrace the sexual meaning of their bodies. John Paul notes that our sexual bodies are "dual" by nature. By this he meant they are made to be given as a gift to someone of the opposite sex. Celibate people cannot give their bodies to someone in a sexual way, of course, but they can give their bodies as gifts in other meaningful ways, serving and loving others tangibly and non-sexually. By choosing celibacy, singles are not renouncing the fundamental meaning of sexuality; they are simply expressing it differently.

SACRAMENTAL UNDERSTANDING AND SEX ROLES IN THE CHURCH

A sacramental understanding of marriage and family has profound implications for sex roles in the church. Again, instead of focusing on what men and women can and can't do, we need to discern the answer to the larger question: Why did God ordain different roles in the church for different genders? As I mentioned earlier, complementarians historically have based distinctions in men's and women's roles in the created order.[33] As Genesis clearly explains, God created man first and then the woman. This order appears significant because it is reiterated in the New Testament as a basis for sex roles. For example, in 1 Corinthians 11:7–8 the apostle Paul instructs women to cover their heads while prophesying or praying, but not men because "man was not made from woman, but woman from man." Again, in 1 Timothy 2:12–14, Paul states that women should not "exercise authority over a man" because "Adam was formed first, then Eve."

However, complementarians rarely mention men's and women's distinct symbolic functions as a rationale for sex roles in the church. This symbolism, though, is implicit in the New Testament text, namely that the church is a family with both mothers and fathers. In 1 Timothy 3:2, for example, Paul says that an overseer in the church should be "the husband of one wife." Then he adds, "He must manage his own household well . . . for if someone does not know how to manage his own household, how will he care for God's church?"[34] Clearly Paul regarded overseers as fathers and saw consistency between a father's leadership role in the home and a spiritual father's leadership role in the church, which is God's family. Paul assumed this paternal role himself, referring to the Corinthian believers as his "beloved children," and writing, "I became your father in Christ Jesus through the gospel."[35]

So it seems that our symbolically important roles in the home have corollaries in the church. Just as men should serve as fathers in the home, men should serve as overseers in the church. This isn't because women can't preach, teach, or lead or are deficient in some way. It's because men and women have different—and equally critical—symbolic roles.

Men are the fathers of the church. Women are the mothers. Both are necessary. Both are God-ordained. Neither is interchangeable.

Reflecting on this truth, noted Christian author C. S. Lewis wrote:

> The kind of equality which implies that the equals are interchangeable (like counters or identical machines) is, among humans, a legal fiction. It may be a useful legal fiction. But in church we turn our back on fictions. One of the ends for which sex was created was to symbolize to us the hidden things of God. One of the functions of human marriage is to express the nature of the union between Christ and the Church. We have no authority to take the living and semitive figures which God has painted on the canvas of our nature and shift them about as if they were mere geometrical figures.[36]

Lewis further argued that fatherhood is inherently spiritual because God is our father, and priests (as spiritual fathers) represent God to the congregation. So placing a spiritual mother in the role of a spiritual father could lead to profound symbolic confusion and spiritual damage: "With the Church . . . we are dealing with male and female not merely as facts of nature but as the live and awful shadows of realities utterly beyond our control and largely beyond our direct knowledge. Or rather, we are not dealing with them but (as we shall soon learn if we meddle) they are dealing with us."[37]

Again, I think complementarians get it right and wrong when it comes to sex roles in the church. I believe they are correct to insist that men exclusively hold the position of priest or pastor. This is crucial for maintaining proper gendered symbolism in the church. However, I think they err when they ban women from preaching, teaching, and fully exercising spiritual gifts. Lewis had no problem with women preaching and teaching, even though he clearly held a complementarian view. He noted that in Scripture, "the same man [Philip the evangelist] had four daughters, virgins, which did prophesy [that is, preached]."[38] What Lewis objected to was women doing "the rest of the priest's work"—things like officiating Communion or performing baptisms. This is where symbolism matters most. In Communion, for example, the pastor presides over the table, breaks the bread, and distributes the wine as Jesus did at the Last Supper. Whether our church tradition recognizes it or not, the pastor serving Communion represents Christ to the congregation, so I think it's legitimate that these functions be reserved for men.

However, the biblical support for barring women from preaching and teaching is rather flimsy. There is only one passage in the New Testament that seemingly forbids women from teaching men—1 Timothy 2:12. As explained on page 11, the passage contains a word that appears only once in Scripture and has dubious meaning, and to interpret this passage as banning women from teaching men seems to contradict other passages where women clearly instructed men. In addition to Philip's daughters, Priscilla, Aquila's wife, instructed Apollos.[39] Biblical scholars continue to debate this point and probably will never settle the matter. I would suggest that a church leadership model that reserves the senior pastorate or priesthood for men, yet allows women subordinate teaching and preaching roles, is about as true to the biblical model as we can reproduce in our contemporary church structures.

Author and speaker Frederica Mathewes-Green explains that her Orthodox church operates this way: Though the denomination maintains an all-male priesthood and has actual patriarchs, its priests are primarily ministers of the sacraments. Nonsacramental ministry, such as preaching, is completely open to laypeople. As a result, Mathewes-Green says her gifts have found greater acceptance in the Orthodox church than in even the mainline Protestant church she used to attend. "I've been welcomed to speak in pulpits and parish halls, and invited to write for Orthodox magazines and book publishers, much more than I ever was in that mainline denomination," she wrote.[40]

I have also seen this model work beautifully in my Anglican church. Though only men can serve as priests, women are welcomed to serve as deacons and even share the pulpit on occasion. But it's not so much what men and women do at my church that makes it special; it's the way that they do it. The male leaders cherish the women not because they can perform like men, but because they contribute something uniquely feminine to the body of believers. When our priest senses that our congregation needs to hear from its spiritual mothers, he will invite several mature women to speak or pray during a service. This kind of deference and respect has engendered a unique reciprocal love and admiration between men and women in our congregation. Perhaps because it represents a mystery hidden in God, this mutuality is hard to describe but provides a taste of triune love. It is, I believe, how God intended men and women to reflect Him in the church. It is extremely compelling but, sadly, extremely rare.

EMBRACING A NEW VISION

Discovering the vision articulated in the Theology of the Body truly transformed my marriage and ministry. It didn't instantly resolve conflicts my husband and I had or dictate how we were to function, but it provided us with a compelling vision that encouraged both of us to love each other sacrificially. The power struggle that sometimes crept into our relationship diminished. Our intimacy increased. And as we began to embrace and celebrate our differences, we grew in our understanding of God and His love.

Similarly TOB gave me a vision of men and women serving together in the church that affirmed women's God-given gifts yet preserved our God-given distinctiveness. This resolved an incredible amount of angst and frustration for me, and it finally put to rest my fears that God was somehow a misogynist. For the first time I understood His vision for men and women, and I found it extremely attractive. Plus, being in a church that reflected this beautiful vision healed wounds that had festered for decades. I began to see the beauty of masculinity and femininity working together in concert, and I began to embrace my unique role as a woman in a greater way than I had before.

Getting to this point, however, took years, and before I could fully embrace this beautiful vision of unity between men and women, I needed to understand the essence of masculinity and femininity and how these qualities could be embodied and expressed in individual persons. Unfortunately the images of manhood and womanhood I too often saw communicated in the church reduced men and women to one-dimensional gendered caricatures, and I had little interest in becoming like one of those. But when I properly understood womanhood in a deeper and more nuanced way, it became attractive and attainable.

Grasping this vision helped me become the woman God had created me to be.

FOUR

A MAN IN EVERY WOMAN
AND A WOMAN IN EVERY MAN

Brandan Robertson and I have a pretty unlikely relationship. Brandan is a Christian LGBTQ activist who identifies as queer. I am a conservative Christian writer and media personality who upholds an orthodox, or historically established, Christian sexual ethic. One might expect us to be adversaries, yet sometimes relationships transcend political and theological barriers. To date, my budding friendship with Brandan has.

Though Brandan is a graduate of the Moody Bible Institute and I work for Moody Radio, we actually never met during his time at Moody. Instead we met at the National Religious Broadcasters Convention in 2015, soon after Brandan had graduated. Brandan was on a panel concerning whether the LGBTQ issue is a salvation issue. As an observer, I felt sorry for him. He was half the age of most of the other panelists and surrounded by hundreds of religious broadcasters, most of whom strongly disagreed with him. Though the panelists were gracious, some of the questions posed were pretty combative, and I imagined that Brandan felt attacked. I imagined correctly.

Afterward, when I met Brandan and expressed sympathy for his situation, he surprised me with a big hug. I asked if I could pray for him, he consented, and ever since I've felt a great deal of warmth toward Brandan. He and I have connected twice over coffee. Despite our differences in theology and age and our short time spent together, we're able to talk honestly and deeply. And yes, we go there—discussing gay issues and what Scripture has to say about sexuality and gender. That's one of the things I appreciate about Brandan. He is willing to wrestle with the Bible and the hard questions. And, though we disagree, we both listen and relate to each other as people, not as representatives of a camp or a side.

So, when I read an article Brandan wrote about biblical manhood—or rather, how he failed to measure up to common notions of biblical manhood—my heart broke. The manhood upheld by the church Brandan attended in high school made him feel insufficient and inferior. To his church, masculinity amounted to controlling one's emotions, excelling in sports, engaging in manual labor, and loving rock music. But that's not Brandan. He's a sweet, soft-spoken man who cries when he's sad, enjoys intellectual rather than physical pursuits, and prefers classical music to rock and roll. "According to many in my community," Brandan wrote, "I was failing to live up to God's standard. I was shamed by my pastor for doing 'sissy work' when I wanted to be in the office instead of outside doing manual labor. My youth pastor made me leave a funeral service because I was crying. He told me, 'If you want to be a pastor, you've got to learn to be a man. Men don't cry.'"[1]

How sad, I thought. Here's a guy who didn't grow up in a Christian home. In fact Brandan's dad was an alcoholic, and his home life was really difficult. Then, when Brandan found Jesus and was assimilated into a church, he was asked to become a masculine caricature rather than being affirmed for the wonderful man God designed him to be. No wonder he rejected what the traditional church told him about sexuality and gender. What a travesty that the church, rather than helping Brandan discover his true self, actually obscured it and wounded him.

As I've participated in scores of churches over the years, I have found that Brandan's experience is not uncommon—nor is it confined to men. Many men, especially sensitive or nonathletic men, struggle to live up to the church's ideal of manhood. But Christian women struggle to live up to the church's ideal of womanhood too. I know I did. I never felt as though I could become the stereotypical Proverbs 31 Woman upheld in so many churches. I was expected to be meek and mild, but I was outspoken and bold and forever feeling as if I didn't fit the model of biblical womanhood. When I read Proverbs 31:10–30, though, the woman described there didn't seem much like the feminine caricature taught in many churches. The Proverbs 31 Woman seemed capable and smart—working vigorously, feeding the poor, making and selling clothes, dispensing wisdom, and managing the affairs of her household. Somehow the more masculine traits of this biblical woman have gotten lost in translation. As a result, many women feel like misfits and woefully inadequate.

Recently, I was surprised to discover that even Kristen Wolfe, a former Miss USA, admitted that she struggled to emulate the Proverbs 31 Woman. "In my mind, the Proverbs 31 Woman was meek, demure, maternal, and perfectly put together—like a sort of Sunday school teacher meets Stepford wife," Wolfe wrote on her blog. "I felt like my feisty, outspoken personality, proclivity for passionate debate, and tendency toward frumpy attire disqualified me from ever being a Proverbs 31 Woman."[2]

Many women I meet in the church—even the most feminine and genteel among us—feel inadequate. I wouldn't be surprised if the same holds true for Christian men. Both sexes suffer from trying to live up to an unrealistic and, I would argue, unhealthy masculine or feminine ideal. Plus, we're confused by the contradictory messages advanced in the church and culture. The culture and many egalitarian or feminist churches try to form women to be like men. And they tell men, in the words of conservative radio host Dennis Prager, "to be ashamed of their masculine natures and to reject masculine virtues."[3] Meanwhile many traditional or complementarian churches advocate the exact opposite—admonishing women to suppress every masculine impulse and men to suppress anything remotely feminine. So men and women are often caught between two extremes and are not terribly excited about embracing either.

Brandan resolved this conflict by diminishing the significance of gender distinctions altogether. "As I have begun to engage the topic of biblical manhood in depth, it's become clear to me that there is no clear set of biblical guidelines for what it means to be a man," he wrote. "Instead, the Bible offers a number of guidelines for how to be a healthy and faithful human being, regardless of one's gender identity. . . . So for followers of Christ, the question should not be what does it look like to be a 'biblical man' or 'biblical woman,' but what does it look like to be fully and truly 'me.'"[4]

Certainly there is truth in what Brandan wrote. We are more than our genders, and gender is not the most important human characteristic. The most fundamental part of our identities as believers is that we are new creations in Christ, a reality that transcends gender, race, class, and any other identity marker we might have. After all, the apostle Paul said that in Christ, "there is neither Jew nor Gentile . . . nor is there male and female."[5] He didn't mean that all our ethnic or gender distinctions are erased when we become Christians. In Revelation 7:9, for example, Scripture offers a glimpse of the multitude in heaven and notes that it includes those "from every nation, tribe, people and language" (NIV). If ethnic distinctions remain after we become believers, then so do our gender distinctions. In fact, one could argue that gender distinctions are far more fundamental than ethnic distinctions because God created us male and female while our ethnic distinctions were not part of the created order but simply developed over time.

Contrary to Brandan's conclusion, asking what it looks like to be a "biblical man" or a "biblical woman" is valid. What are not valid are the caricatures we have come to accept in the church. They are not biblical models but composites of select scriptures and a false cultural narrative. True masculine and feminine, though obviously expressed in culturally relevant ways, actually transcend culture. They are more profound than displaying a certain personality type or playing sports. They are expressions of God.

GENDER AS TWIN REFLECTIONS OF GOD

Our culture uses sex and gender somewhat interchangeably, and to a certain extent, that is valid. If someone asks what gender someone is, we commonly reply male or female, referring to the person's biological sex. Yet technically *gender* refers to something beyond biology. According to Christian author and psychology professor Mark Yarhouse, gender is "the psychological, social and cultural aspects of being male and female."[6] To him and most of the psychological and social science community, gender refers to the roles and behaviors that culture assigns each sex, as well as the ways men and women commonly perceive themselves.

As I mentioned in chapter 3, C. S. Lewis suggested that gender is not a creation of culture but culture's way of expressing a transcendent reality present in God's creation. Lewis eloquently expressed this idea in *Perelandra*, the second book of his space trilogy. In this science fiction novel, the main character, Ransom, encounters the ruling angels of Malacandra (Mars) and Perelandra (Venus). Although these angels have no sexual characteristics, Ransom perceives them as undoubtedly "masculine (not male)" and "feminine (not female)." This gendered reality, despite the absence of anatomical sex, reveals a profound truth, as the book's narrator explains:

> What Ransom saw in that moment was the real meaning of gender. Everyone must sometimes have wondered why in nearly all tongues certain inanimate objects are masculine and others feminine. What is masculine about a mountain or feminine about certain trees? Ransom has cured me of believing that this is a purely morphological phenomenon, depending on the form of the word. Still less is gender an imaginative extension of sex. Our ancestors did not make mountains masculine because they projected male characteristics into them. The real process is the reverse. Gender is a reality and a more fundamental reality than sex. Sex is, in fact, merely the adaptation to organic life of a fundamental polarity which divides all created beings. Female sex is simply one of the things which has feminine gender; there are many others and Masculine and Feminine meet us on planes of reality where male and female would be simply meaningless. Masculine is not attenuated male, nor feminine attenuated female. On the contrary, the male and female of organic creatures are rather faint and blurred reflections of masculine and feminine.[7]

So to Lewis, who provided some of the most profound insights on this subject, gender is a permanent reality inherent in the material world and existing above and beyond it. It is expressed in human culture, but it also transcends culture. The reason for this, Lewis intimated, is that gender reveals attributes of God.

The idea that gender expressed qualities inherent in God was novel to me before I became acquainted with healing ministry, but it immediately resonated with me. Leanne Payne, who was also a C. S. Lewis scholar, wrote, "Sexuality and gender are grounded in the Being of God and His creation. Masculinity and femininity, rooted in God, have utterly transcendent dimensions."[8] This idea rang true to me. If God made us in His image, then it seemed likely that our masculinity and femininity, so integral to who we are as persons, might be reflections of Him.

But what are masculinity and femininity? Certainly some notions of masculine and feminine are socially constructed and vary from culture to culture. Though they may be people's unconscious expressions of something transcendent and real, there's no doubt that humans tend to distort and imperfectly reflect spiritual realities. Yet if gender is actually rooted in God, then there must exist masculine and feminine qualities that are essential and unchanging. And if, as John Paul II taught, our bodies are a living theology, then the clues to the essence of masculinity and femininity should be stamped on our bodies. And they are.

Karl Stern, a psychiatrist and convert from Judaism to Christianity, noted this in his book *The Flight from Woman*, "In the act of sexual union, the male sex organ is convex and penetrating and the female organ is concave and receptive; the spermatozoon is torpedo-shaped and attacks, and the ovum is a sphere 'awaiting' penetration."[9] These physical differences are not merely external but reflect profound differences in the souls of men and women. As theologian Emil Brunner wrote, "Our sexuality penetrates to the deepest metaphysical ground of our personality. As a result, the physical differences between the man and the woman are a parable of the psychical and spiritual differences of a more ultimate nature."[10] Explaining this "parable" further, Stern wrote, "Just as in sexual physiology, the female principle is one of receiving, keeping and nourishing."[11] Likewise, the masculine principle is one of action—of moving into the world and ordering—or, as famed missionary and Christian author Elisabeth Elliot taught, the "distilled essence of masculinity" is initiation,[12] and the essence of femininity is response.[13]

These essential masculine and feminine characteristics are also profoundly expressed in the creation account. Genesis tells us that God created man first and placed him in the garden of Eden "to work it and keep it."[14] He also assigned to man the task of naming the animals. Theologians have long held that this delegation of responsibility was not arbitrary but correlated to the essence of masculinity, which involves initiation, work (provision), and order. God's curse for Adam's sin is not arbitrary either, but strikes at the very core of his masculinity—his ability to order and subdue creation: "Cursed is the ground because of you . . . Thorns and thistles it shall bring forth for you . . . By the sweat of your face / you shall eat bread."[15] As a result of the Fall, man would be frustrated when trying to exercise his masculinity. His initiative would be blocked by creation itself.

Scripture says God created the woman, on the other hand, to be a feminine complement to the man. She is his "helper."[16] Much has been made about the Hebrew word *ezer*, which is translated "helper" in most modern Bible translations. Some complementarians, or traditionalists, say woman's creation as a "helper" means she is subordinate to man and created to function "as a loyal and suitable assistant."[17] Though I believe in male headship, I don't believe that is what ezer communicates in Genesis 2. Here God is not communicating authority but necessity and complementarity. In fact, ezer in the rest of the

Old Testament refers to the assistance someone stronger, such as God or a king, offers to someone in need.[18] Ezer communicates that man needs woman. She gives something unique that is essential to him, so without her he is incomplete.

Dr. John McKinley, an author and professor of biblical and theological studies at Biola University, stresses this point, suggesting that "necessary ally" is a better translation of ezer than "helper." "The issue in ezer is neither equality nor subordination, but distinction and relatedness," he writes. "She is to be for the man as an ally to benefit him in the work they were given to do. . . . What sort of ally is the woman to the man? She is a necessary ally, the sort without which he cannot fulfill humanity's mission."[19] The woman provides the necessary complement to the man's action-oriented masculinity. The essence of her femininity is response and nurture—the very things necessary to sustain life and relationships. Without her, humanity ends with Adam. But with her, Adam and Eve are able to be fruitful and multiply.

As with the man, God's curse for Eve's sin strikes at the core of her femininity: her ability to work harmoniously with Adam and to bear children. Adam will now "rule over" her—and the product of their union, children, will now be born "in pain."[20]

These two essential qualities—masculinity and femininity—are found not just in man and woman, but also in God. In creation, for example, we see an awesome display of masculinity as God speaks the entire universe into existence. Yet in passages such as Isaiah 66:13, God displays feminine characteristics, too, saying, "As a mother comforts her child, / so will I comfort you" (NIV). Similarly in Luke 13:34, Jesus laments, "Jerusalem, Jerusalem, you who kill the prophets and stone those sent to you, how often I have longed to gather your children together, as a hen gathers her chicks under her wings, and you were not willing" (NIV).

God is never referred to in Scripture as mother, but only as Father. Similarly Jesus is never called the daughter of man, but only the Son of man. He likewise is called our bridegroom, and we are the bride. This masculine imagery for God and feminine imagery for us are appropriate because God, our Creator and Savior, always initiates, leaving us only to respond. As Elliot wrote, "All creation responds to His initiating. It is the only thing creation can do."[21] Or, echoing the same sentiments, Lewis wrote in *That Hideous Strength*, "What is above and beyond all things is so masculine that we are all feminine in relation to it."[22]

So gender, like sex and marriage, is highly symbolic and helps us understand the nature of God and how we relate to Him. Gender, sex, and marriage are integral to each other and to the image of God reflected in us. Dr. Wayne Martindale, C. S. Lewis scholar and professor emeritus of English at Wheaton College, wrote explicitly about this gendered symbolism:

> Did this problem of knowing God and how human beings would refer to Him and think of Him escape God in the creation of gender? Or did He create a system which would adequately allow for us to conceptualize and talk about Him, and did He give us a divine revelation of the imagery we should use? Is it not more credible, given the supreme importance of knowing God rightly, that He should, in fact, create gender for the purpose of revelation?[23]

Gender is not in any way arbitrary or bound by culture. It is an enduring reflection of our unchanging God, and it is something that we, as masculine and feminine bearers of the divine image, have a responsibility to properly embody and express.

A MAN IN EVERY WOMAN AND A WOMAN IN EVERY MAN

Recently I had the privilege of emceeing a portion of the Pastors' Conference at the Moody Bible Institute. To my knowledge, I was the first woman to ever appear on the stage at one of these annual events, and to my delight, the male pastors and a handful of female spouses and church leaders were very welcoming. I had a wonderful experience. However, a few men at the conference felt uncomfortable with my presence. On one occasion, I overheard a gentleman arguing with several others in the hallway, saying, "Women should not be allowed to do that."

Others, I detected, didn't have any theological problem with a woman emceeing a conference, even a pastors' conference. They simply didn't know how to respond to a woman in an up-front role. Before one of the sessions, it was my job to throw free T-shirts and hats, bound by rubber bands, into the audience. Afterward, while I was talking to one gentleman, two other men came up and jokingly remarked, "Hey, we noticed you don't throw like a girl!" I smiled and thought, *I was a Little League pitcher. Of course I don't throw like a girl!* But the gentleman to whom I was talking said, "Yes, you do! Listen, there's nothing wrong with being like a girl—and you're just fine."

I think he meant what he said as a compliment. And it kind of was. I mean, I was glad he thought I was adequately feminine. So what if I throw like a boy? Does that somehow make me less of a woman? I smiled and dismissed the comment. But the interaction reminded me of how weird people in the church can be when it comes to gender issues, and how one-dimensional we often are in our thinking. This is why I appreciate what Lewis and Payne contribute to the gender conversation. They remind us of God's complexity and urge us to think in a nuanced way about men and women as complex beings.

Reflecting on God's possession of both masculine and feminine characteristics, Leanne Payne wrote, "We, in His image, are most surely—in our spiritual, psychological, and physical beings—bipolar creatures. Our Creator, holding all that is true and real within himself, reflects both the masculine and the feminine, and so do we."[24] In other words, there's nothing wrong with a woman having some masculine characteristics or a man having feminine characteristics. In fact, it's healthy and appropriately reflects our Maker. I think most of us intuitively get this concept. No one likes a man who is devoid of feminine characteristics and unable to show any compassion or tenderness. Similarly no one likes a woman who is "sickly passive,"[25] as Payne puts it, and unable to say no or to exert her will. C. S. Lewis expressed this sentiment well in a letter to his lifelong friend and correspondent, Sister Penelope. "There ought spiritually to be a man in every woman and a woman in every man," he wrote. "And how horrid the ones who haven't got it are: I can't bear a 'man's man' or a 'woman's woman.'"[26] Here Lewis and Payne are not advocating for androgyny or gender ambiguity. Men should still be masculine and women should be feminine. They're simply saying men and women should have some balance.

This has a strong theological basis in the creation account in Genesis. God did not create Eve from the dust as He did Adam; Eve is formed from the rib of the man. So, as theologian Paul Evdokimov profoundly noted, "The creation of Eve is not a 'creation,' but a real birth; Eve is separated from Adam." This is significant because it implies that before Eve's creation—or birth—"Adam already contained in himself his constituent part, his 'other half,' Eve." This interpretation is supported by the Hebrew words in this passage. The word used for Adam in his initial creation is *adam*, which according to Evdokimov means mankind, or man "in the collective sense." Initially Adam is not a differentiated, gendered person but represents all of humanity, both male and female. After Eve's creation in Genesis 2:21–22, man is referred to as *ish* (male-man) and woman is referred to as *ishah* (female-man). When Adam looks at Eve, he doesn't refer to her as other but sees his mirror image: "bone of my bones and flesh of my flesh" (Gen. 2:23). Eve is a complement to Adam, but she is also like him and he like her.[27]

Anatomically Eve is similar to Adam. In fact, the sex organs of men have their rudimentary complement in women and vice versa. It's as though the man retains part of the woman in himself and the woman part of the man, yet each in a degree appropriate to his or her sex. Would it not also make sense that men and women embody both masculine and feminine in a degree appropriate to their sexes? Payne explicitly proposed this idea. "The more nearly we function in (God's) image," she wrote, "the more nearly we reflect both the masculine and the feminine in their proper balance—that is, in the differing degrees and aptitudes appropriate to our sexual identities as male and female."[28] For a woman to be healthy, she not only needs to embrace her feminine—to be free to hear and receive from God—but she also needs to embrace the masculine and be empowered to respond in the way God leads.

Philosopher and theologian Alice von Hildebrand expressed this concept well. "Great female saints," she once said, "while keeping the perfume of female gentleness, can show a strength and courage that sociology usually reserves to the male sex. It is typical of the supernatural that such apparently contradictory features can be harmoniously united."[29] The same holds true for men. To be healthy, a man not only needs to embrace his masculine drive to initiate and create, but he also needs to embrace the feminine so he can listen and respond to God and others.

This paradigm opened me up to a new way of living, where I focused less on what I do and more on who I should become—a healthy reflection of God, responding appropriately to these movements in my soul. Before this point I constantly felt as if I were supposed to suppress my masculine traits. I can even remember being told in a women's class at church that wives should not air their opinions or ever take initiative in their homes. If we did, the Bible teacher warned, our husbands would never lead. Of course, if we dominate our husbands, then we may need healing and strengthening in our feminine capacity to receive and nurture. Those of us women who possess strong masculine gifts need to also have well-developed feminine sides to avoid becoming imbalanced. If our strengths intimidate our husbands or other men in our lives, then these men may need healing and strengthening in their masculinity. The solution to our unhealthy imbalances, for both men and women, is to bless and affirm what is weak or estranged rather than to weaken and suppress what is holy and good.

This process of listening and responding to the Holy Spirit as He illumines and works in our souls is more organic and fluid than many Christian communities allow. They prefer the very clear and well-regimented imposition of roles, so when they find a square peg—a man or woman who is not healthy in his or her masculinity or femininity—they try to fix this person by informing him or her of proper sex roles. Sometimes these roles aren't even accurate and are ideals formed more by culture than by Scripture. For example, Scripture does not say men must enjoy sports or women should have demure personalities. Even when the roles we try to impose are biblical, forcing square pegs into round holes is painful and futile. Rather than trying to get people to conform externally, Christian communities need to foster environments where people heal and grow. They need to model healthy masculinity and femininity in its various forms, and then help men and women respond to the Holy Spirit as He brings to life what needs to be nurtured and blessed. As we do this in community, people blossom and grow and more beautifully and accurately reflect God to the world.

I was fortunate that when I was processing what it meant to be a woman, I had a healthy community of Christians around me. They modeled healthy masculine and feminine natures, and they affirmed what was good and healthy in me while patiently addressing what needed to change. I would not be the person I am today without their wise and gentle leadership in my life. I wish more people had nurturing experiences like mine, rather than the wounding and demeaning experience Brandan had in his church. The church must become a place where people can discover and become their true selves, not personalities made in the image of culture or caricatures of the church, but in the image of God.

This is perhaps more crucial now than it ever has been at any time in history. Satan is well aware of how critical healthy sexuality and gender are to our spiritual well-beings, and that may be why he has been steadily assaulting and perverting them ever since he met Adam and Eve in the garden. Today we are aiding Satan in his assault. He has deceived us and caused us to hate and reject essential parts of ourselves, and the result is breathtakingly awful.

FIVE

ANDROGYNY,
THE NEW MISOGYNY

"The happiest day of my life was when they said, 'It's a boy!'" That one comment, uttered by her father in front of a group at church, altered the course of Janet's[1] life. Today Janet is a friend and colleague at Moody Radio, and she recently told me her story when I visited her at home. At the time her father made that statement, she was just twelve years old and desperate to win her father's love and attention, which her younger brother, Skip, seemed to enjoy.

When he was angry with her, her father would yank her hair, slap her face, or play a sadistic game where he'd push her little finger into her hand until she was writhing on the floor. Because of these treatments, though, Janet learned at an early age that performance could sometimes win her what she desperately craved. She became an extremely high achiever, scoring at the top of her class and winning school competitions. But her father's comment that day dashed her hopes of ever truly winning his unconditional love and affirmation.

"What has Skip done?" she recalled thinking. "I make A's. I've won art contests. [I play] the flute. I've done all this stuff. . . . Just because he's a boy?" In that moment, Janet said she realized that no matter what grades she achieved or awards she accumulated, her father would always value her less because she was female. From that day forward, she saw her femininity as a vice, not a virtue.

Other dysfunctions in Janet's home reinforced this rejection of the feminine. When she was about seven, she found pornography in her father's drawer. She vividly remembers seeing the cover of a *Hustler* magazine depicting a woman's legs coming out of the top of a meat grinder. "At the time that I saw that," she said, "I couldn't put together the horror that that particular cover was conveying in objectifying women. I just remember the sight. . . . When you're young, it doesn't really register, but there's something at the very gut level of the soul that is shaken."

Janet also internalized her father's devaluation of her mother, who was a stay-at-home mom. "I didn't see a lot of respect for what my mother did," she said. "In fact, I saw a lot of devaluing of who she was as a person." Janet said her father would say things like, "Barb, just shut up and put the dinner on the table!" Or, he'd often use profanity in conjunction with her mother's name. "God-dammit, Barb!" was a frequently heard phrase. "I always thought that God's middle name was dammit and his last name was Barb," Janet joked. But the pain she felt as a child was no laughing matter.

Given the way her father treated her mother, Janet had no desire to grow up, find a husband, and replay her mother's fate. After graduating from high school, she secured a near-full scholarship to Wheaton College—not the evangelical flagship in Illinois, but the secular and very liberal formerly all-women's private college in Massachusetts. There, Janet's rejection of feminine things, which had been largely subconscious, became overt and focused. At Wheaton her anger toward her father, and toward men in general, was stoked into a raging fire.

During orientation week, Janet and her entire class were shown a documentary exploring the fate of Rosie the Riveter, who represented the millions of women who worked in factories and shipyards during World War II. Near the end of the movie, when the soldiers are returning home, a reporter asks one of these women how she feels about relinquishing her job to a man. This "Rosie" replied in a Southern accent that she was "so happy to give up her job for a boy who's returning home." At this, the entire auditorium erupted in boos and protest. The women at Wheaton were angry at men, and their revenge was going to be independence secured by successful careers. Janet quickly embraced this attitude and, fed with a constant stream of feminist literature, became convinced that "housewives and mothers—women who stayed at home—were the most miserable group among women of all occupations."

Janet's anger toward men continued to simmer throughout her four years of college and for at least a decade afterward. She became increasingly estranged from her emotions and tried to avoid her feelings. "My emotions remained a very neglected area of my life," she said. "If I could have been Vulcan, I would have chosen that. Feelings were an inconvenience." Janet also suffered from chronic depression, which was often triggered by failure to meet her perfectionist standards. "I would beat myself up if I perceived I failed," she said. "I had one of these episodes when I got a quarterly average of 99 in English. I was upset I hadn't gotten a 100 average, which I had achieved both before and after the fact."

For the first decade after graduating from college, Janet remained single and pursued her career goals. In what seemed like a fluke, she got a job at a Christian radio station and eventually became the manager there. Janet had become a Christian as a child, but she had never really matured in her faith. Listening to the preaching at the station helped her grow in her understanding of God. Still her faith remained largely in her head. "[God] was a father who was way away. Where was He?" she said. "God, for me at the time . . . was just another professor, you know, with more homework assignments—like praying. I didn't feel God's love. Everything I knew was intellectual."

At age thirty-five Janet got married, despite her ambivalence toward men. This resulted in a tumultuous courtship and early years of marriage. Her estrangement from her own sex also made having children a terrifying prospect. "I had this fear, again, of being my mom—of being trapped," she said. "And by then, I didn't really like kids. I don't mean I disliked them. It just wasn't like, 'I want to be a mom.'"

Instead of having kids, Janet became the first woman to manage a Moody Radio owned-and-operated station. She got a doctorate and eventually was invited to join the Moody Radio Network management team. She continued to battle depression, and her relationship with God remained rote. She experienced growth in her attitudes about men—specifically her husband—but the wounds from her childhood remained unhealed and her estrangement from her emotions and her gender persisted.

MISOGYNY—A COMMON MALADY

Though Janet's story is unique, her misogyny is not. The word *misogyny* comes from the Greek *misos*, meaning "hatred," and *gyne*, meaning "woman." People often use this term quite literally to mean "hatred of women." Feminists are often the ones who recognize and denounce misogyny, pointing to its clear manifestations in the rampant physical and sexual abuse of women, the sexual objectification of women, and discrimination against women in the workplace. These overt manifestations of misogyny are devastating to women and should be strongly opposed.

Before participating in a healing program, though, I had never really considered that women could be misogynists, that we can internalize the misogyny we have received and actually despise and suppress uniquely feminine aspects in ourselves. We might reject uniquely feminine roles, such as motherhood, as Janet had done. Or, we might embrace and value traditionally masculine traits, including power, reason, and initiative, while spurning traditionally feminine ones, such as tenderness, emotion, and intuition. This more subtle form of misogyny manifests as a hatred of the feminine—of what women uniquely contribute and represent. Ironically feminists who are supposed to promote women are some of the worst perpetrators of this type of misogyny.

Dr. Larry Crabb explained how this can happen in his book *Men and Women: Enjoying the Difference.* "A common solution to the problem of inescapable pain in our masculine and feminine souls is to anesthetize the part of our being that has been most deeply hurt," he wrote. "We therefore cut off from our own awareness what is most thoroughly male or female about us. By ceasing to exist as a man or woman and reducing ourselves to the safer existence of neutered personhood, we are able to face life as intact persons less threatened and more confident."[2] Few go so far as to actually become "neutered persons," at least physically, but many women devalue, despise, or reject aspects of their womanhood.

For some women, such as Janet, this is the result of personal wounding. Someone close to them devalued, cursed, or even abused their feminine natures, making them want to shed those parts of themselves to gain acceptance. This often happens subconsciously. The victims aren't intentionally rejecting their feminine; the feminine has come to symbolize something negative to them, so they have developed an aversion to feminine qualities.

For others this rejection of the feminine is the result of internalizing the misogynistic values prevalent in our culture. When I was a child, for example, it was okay for a young girl to dream of becoming a wife and stay-at-home mom. Many of us still wanted to get educations and pursue career goals, but putting those on hold for a family was socially acceptable. Now the reverse is true. Girls are conditioned to want careers above all else. Having a husband and family is okay, but not at the expense of one's career. Similarly, girls today are encouraged to be strong—to fight for themselves rather than to wait for a knight in shining armor. I'm somewhat amused by fight scenes common in movies and TV today that regularly feature women beating up on men. The cultural message is that power is a desirable virtue; meekness and gentleness are not.

Like many women, I never would have dreamed that I harbored misogynistic attitudes. I felt a deep affinity with those of my gender and wanted to promote the interests of women as much as possible. But in the late nineties, as I was working through some of the issues that led to my codependency, I attended a conference sponsored by Ministries of Pastoral Care—a ministry founded by Leanne Payne. There I was introduced to the many ways misogyny can manifest. At first it was purely academic to me. Then, during a session Payne was leading, I began to have a visceral response to her. Now deceased, Payne was in her late sixties at the time and was grandmotherly in her delivery. She would often refer to the audience as "dear ones" and would speak to us in soft and tender tones. She also communicated poetically, which irritated me. I wanted her to communicate concepts efficiently and succinctly. As I listened to her, my frustration turned to disgust, and I began to ruminate about how much I disliked her. She was too sweet, too soft-spoken, too—something I couldn't quite put my finger on. Then it hit me. She was too feminine.

That was an epiphany. I realized at the time that disliking some-one simply because she was extremely feminine was not good. I was in a period of healing and self-reflection, so I naturally began examining why I would have such a negative response to someone simply because she was feminine. Over the next several days and weeks, I realized that I associated certain feminine characteristics with weakness. I thought weakness was what allowed men to dominate and dismiss women, so it was something I shunned.

I'm sure some of this attitude was formed in my childhood in response to my brother, who was six years older than me. Though I love my brother and we have a good relationship today, when we were young he seemed to delight in bullying my sisters and me. My sisters generally responded by staying out of his way. But I was strong-willed, and my sense of justice was too violated to submit to him. We fought constantly. I always lost, but my losing only strengthened my resolve to resist giving in to him. As I grew older and received more slights and perceived injustices at the hands of other men, this resolve strengthened. By the time of that conference, I was pretty resistant not just to being dominated but to certain aspects of femininity. This, I soon discovered, is not uncommon.

About a year after this epiphany, I was coleading a small group of women in the same healing ministry that I had recently completed. My coleader, Annette, asked the group to name something they loved about being a woman. The women—whose issues ranged from low self-esteem to eating disorders, depression, gender confusion, and sub-stance abuse—responded with blank stares and silence. So Annette rephrased the question: "Okay, name something you like in other women."

After about fifteen seconds, one woman spoke up. "Strength," she said.

"Yeah, strength," said another.

Then a third woman chimed in, "And leadership. I like women who are strong and can lead."

Now the group was beginning to click, and several women began sharing short descriptions of strong, smart female leaders they respected and admired. There's nothing wrong with these kinds of women; I admire them too. Yet conspicuously absent was any mention of characteristics thought of as feminine, such as nurturing, compassion, or tenderness.

My coleader and I mentioned this omission to the group and asked what they thought about it.

The women were silent for a minute or two. Then one said, "I guess I associate tenderness and compassion with weakness."

"Me too," said another. "I've just seen men take advantage of that. I don't want to be those things. It just invites abuse."

The rest of the women expressed similar sentiments and shared stories of ways men had hurt them. Most of these women were feminine in their appearances, yet beneath their pretty and feminine exteriors lay a deep-seated rejection of feminine virtues.

"A WORLD IMPOVERISHED OF WOMANLY VALUES"

About fifty years ago Dr. Karl Stern noted a similar phenomenon among a growing number of patients in his psychiatry practice.

In his book *The Flight from Woman,* Dr. Stern explained that his patients—women and men—increasingly suffered from a rejection of the feminine. This resulted in what he termed the "problem of activism"—a lack of balance between action and contemplation. In men, this problem manifested as an "endless drive and ambition," "a shying away from tenderness," "an extraordinary denial of feeling," "undue intellectualism," and "approaches to human relationships as if they were matters of engineering." In women, the problem manifested as "an over-evaluation of masculine achievement and a debasement of values which one commonly associates with womanly achievement; a rejection, often unconscious, even of motherhood; an aping of man, associated with an unceasing undertone of envy and resentment."[3]

Dr. Stern witnessed that these "abnormalities in character" were more prevalent at the writing of his book (in 1965) than in any other time in history. He observed that this rejection of all things feminine was not just evident on a personal level but on a societal level. In his opinion, never before had a population so thoroughly devalued and rejected the unique contributions of women and the feminine ways of knowing and being. He prophetically lamented "the ghastly spectre of a world impoverished of womanly values."[4] Now, more than fifty years later, this is an accurate description of much of Western society.

There's no doubt that women look and act more like men than we have at any other time in Western history—perhaps in all of history. In the past forty to fifty years, we have relinquished many of the roles and characteristics considered uniquely feminine and acquired many roles and characteristics once considered uniquely or primarily masculine. In 1972, for example, American women represented just 38 percent of the workforce, and nearly half of mothers stayed at home.[5] By 2014 we comprised just under half of the total workforce and more than half of those in professional and technical jobs.[6]

Today less than 30 percent of mothers stay at home,[7] and women are entering jobs that used to be exclusively for men. Perhaps the most radical of these are combat roles in the military. In 2015 the Defense Department opened all military occupations and positions to women, so now we can fight just like men in the infantry, armor, reconnaissance, and even some special operations units.[8]

The radical change has also occurred in the world of athletics. Since 2000 the Olympics have added to women's competition the traditionally male sports of weightlifting, wrestling, and boxing—and female competitors now display bulging biceps and six-pack abs that shame many men. Certainly we have achieved great heights, performing feats never before thought possible.

Breaking these barriers and acquiring masculine characteristics might be okay if women retained feminine qualities. But sports such as gymnastics, which used to value artistry, now reward the most spectacular and athletic twists and tumbles. As one writer mused, "Is it true that the women's floor exercise has transformed from lovely performance art on par with Cirque du Soleil to a graceless exhibition of athleticism at the expense of beauty?"[9]

Women also have appropriated some of men's undesirable qualities, such as aggression and violence. From 1980 to 2010 the percentage of female juvenile arrests for violent crimes rose from 10 to 18 percent; the female percentage of juvenile arrests for aggravated assault alone rose from 15 to 25 percent.[10] But perhaps most stunning, a 2014 study conducted by the Centers for Disease Control and Prevention found that women are now raping men at nearly the same rate as men rape women. This study defined rape broadly to include not just physical domination but other types of coercion, such as "lies or false promises, threats to end a relationship or spread negative gossip or 'making repeated requests' for sex and expressing unhappiness at being turned down."[11] Some may argue that this hardly qualifies as rape, and I would tend to agree with them. Still, the findings are shocking and reveal how some women have become like the most brutish of men in their attitudes concerning sex and children.

Women in previous generations wanted families and saw the link between sex and procreation as a benefit. That link was a way to compel men to take their sexual behavior seriously and to secure a commitment—something men traditionally resisted but women traditionally embraced. Now women have become as sexually libertine as men and view their own natural reproductive functions as a liability. We now demand contraception as a fundamental right and, even more stunning, we participate in the slaughter of our own progeny—something that violates the most fundamental feminine impulse.

There's been no commensurate move by men to become like women or to embrace feminine qualities. They have not, for example, pushed to compete in the all-women's sports of synchronized swimming or rhythmic gymnastics. Men have not abandoned their traditional working roles en masse to replace women as stay-at-home dads, nor has the corporate world become less masculine. In fact, a Stanford study found that women who are masculine (i.e., aggressive, assertive, and confident) do best in the business world (though they also reportedly need to be able to deactivate these traits in certain social situations).[12]

The transition has been almost completely one-sided because society values masculine traits and devalues feminine ones. Women have worked tirelessly to become like men, to shed their feminine and become androgynous. And the home, which once served as the base for women's strong feminine influence, has been largely abandoned and diminished. So the "man's world" remains a man's world, despite being populated with women. And what used to be a "woman's world" is quickly fading—and with it, the feminine presence our society so desperately needs. If imitation is the sincerest form of flattery, we women have greatly flattered men while simultaneously insulting ourselves—and impoverishing our world. We need to recapture what it means to be a woman. And we need to embrace who God made us to be, rather than trying to recreate ourselves as men.

THE NECESSITY OF SELF-ACCEPTANCE

Until I reached my midthirties, I chafed against being a woman. Some of this was innocent; as a kid I found dresses and hose extremely uncomfortable. But as I described, some of it also stemmed from a fundamental rejection of the feminine, which essentially was a rejection of myself. Philosopher and theologian Romano Guardini wrote, "The act of self-acceptance is the root of all things. I must agree to be the person I am. Agree to have the qualifications which I have. Agree to live within the limitations set for me. . . . The clarity and the courageousness of this acceptance is the foundation of all existence."[13]

When God first convicted me of my own misogyny, I realized the attitude was wrong and amounted to rebellion against God. He had intentionally chosen to create me as a woman, so by rejecting the feminine I was rejecting myself, and by extension I was rejecting Him. This, I realized, was a serious offense. Isaiah 45:9–10 says, "Woe to those who quarrel with their Maker, / those who are nothing but potsherds / among the potsherds on the ground. / Does the clay say to the potter, / 'What are you making?' / Does your work say, / 'The potter has no hands'?" (NIV). When I realized what I was doing and simply confessed my sin to God, an amazing thing happened. It didn't happen instantly, but slowly I began to appreciate and even love the feminine. And I began to feel more feminine. When I stopped fighting my own nature and submitted to it, the feminine blossomed. I began to relax and enjoy motherhood more. I stopped chafing against my limitations. I experienced more peace than I had ever experienced before. This happened over a period of years, and in some ways, it is still happening today.

Janet's healing, on the other hand, was more immediate and dramatic. Soon after moving to Chicago to take a management job with the Moody Radio Network, she and her husband began attending the same Anglican church that my family attends. The church is thoroughly evangelical and has a Spirit-led and emotionally expressive worship style. Initially that quality scared Janet, but it also attracted her. She recognized that she needed to grow in her ability to connect with God emotionally, and she figured attending a church with an expressive worship style would help her do that. So she and her husband committed to attending our church. Janet also enrolled in Transformation Intensive, a rigorous, nine-month course of spiritual formation inspired by the sixteenth-century theologian Ignatius of Loyola. During that course, God began transforming Janet's heart.

The course encouraged participants to read and meditate on Scripture and invited them to allow God to speak not only through their rational minds, but also through their imaginations. This was new to Janet, but something she took to naturally. During one session a leader led Janet through a healing prayer where, under the direction of the Holy Spirit, they prayed about her father and her mother and also her spouse. Janet described the evening as moving, but it was only the precursor to the profound work God would do thirty minutes later. As she drove home, she suddenly remembered the hurtful comment her father had made about the happiest day of his life being when they said, "It's a boy!" Janet then began imagining what the day of *her* birth was like. She remembered her mother saying that it was snowing and that her father had been watching *Hogan's Heroes* (a popular CBS sitcom in the sixties and seventies). As she was imagining this, she heard God say to her spirit, "*I* was happy when they said, 'It's a girl!'"

Even as Janet relayed this experience to me months later, she choked up. She said the moment she heard God speak, her emotions unlocked. For decades she had suppressed them because she feared that letting her emotions surface would be too painful. But now she felt she could face the pain of her father's rejection without being overwhelmed, and even feel compassion for him. In that moment she knew her heavenly Father accepted her, which made the hurt by her earthly father bearable. "When you receive affirmation from the Creator of the universe, and *He* expresses joy at what *He* made, and *He* expresses happiness at your birth, that you were born just the way *He* wanted you to be born—when you hear that from the God of the universe, who's sovereign over everything, that's the period on the end of the sentence." And indeed, for Janet, it was. For the first time, she was able to embrace that God had created her a woman—and to believe that it was good.

For many women today, both inside the church and outside, this truth and affirmation of their womanhood escape them. Much as Janet was, they are caught up in a feminist movement, which denies their essential natures and encourages them on paths of self-destruction. We need a true feminism—not one that, in the words of feminist icon Gloria Steinem, encourages us to become "the men we wanted to marry."[14] We need a feminism that encourages us to become women of God.

SIX

BEYOND FEMINISM

The 2016 election presented something of a crisis for American feminists. On the cusp of breaking the ultimate glass ceiling—electing Hillary Clinton as the first female president—young Democratic women weren't falling in line. In the primaries these women were largely backing democratic socialist Bernie Sanders, which incensed older feminist stalwarts, such as Madeleine Albright and Gloria Steinem. At a rally in New Hampshire, Albright castigated young women voters, saying, "There's a special place in hell for women who don't help each other!" Steinem expressed similar sentiments and suggested that these young female holdouts simply didn't care about important political issues. In an interview with talk show host Bill Maher, she said, "When you're young, you're thinking: 'Where are the boys? The boys are with Bernie.'"[1]

These statements by these old-guard feminists unleashed an avalanche of criticism. Albright soon apologized for her statement—sort of. "I absolutely believe what I said, that women should help one another," she said, "but this was the wrong context and the wrong time to use that line." She continued, "The battle for gender equality is still being waged, and it will be easier if we have a woman who prioritizes these issues in the Oval Office."[2] Steinem also issued a half-hearted apology, saying she simply "misspoke" and that she didn't mean to imply that "young women aren't serious in their politics." As did Albright, Steinem reaffirmed the message that any self-respecting young woman should affirm feminist ideals. These women should be "mad as hell about what's happening to them," Steinem said, specifically noting that many are "graduating in debt, but averaging a million dollars less over their lifetimes to pay it back."[3]

In the end Clinton clinched the party's nomination, despite weak support from young women. Eventually most feminists, young and old, got behind her candidacy. Young feminists, however, complained that Clinton's second-wave feminism wasn't radical enough and was too privileged and outdated. "It's fine for middle-class white people, but it completely ignores intersectionality," said Erica Brandt, a twenty-seven-year-old who works in education policy. *Intersectionality* is a theory popular among so-called fourth-wave feminists that views oppression and discrimination as the result of intersecting social identities, such as gender, race, class, and sexual orientation. For these feminists Clinton's whiteness and failure to fully support gay marriage before 2013 was a problem. "Gay rights is a huge feminist issue," said twenty-eight-year-old Deva Cats Baril, "and her lack of accountability for not recognizing that before is a problem." Baril, who's part Mexican and part Lebanese, added, "I think the whole pro-Hillary camp of feminism creepily mirrors the larger problems facing feminism today. It's all about uplifting and forgiving white women and entitlement when it comes to positions of power."[4]

Another group of feminists who struggled to come to terms with Clinton were Jesus feminists, like the ones I met when participating in the Moody Radio podcast about women's roles.[5] These

Christian women with feminist convictions were torn. Though they affirmed many of Clinton's feminist ideals, they objected to her radical pro-choice advocacy. In addition to defending late-trimester and even partial-birth abortion,[6] Clinton advocated repealing the Hyde Amendment, which banned the use of taxpayer funds for abortion.[7] For some Jesus feminists, Clinton's support for abortion was a deal breaker. But for others, such as Karisa Johns Smith, a doctoral candidate at an evangelical school, it was not. To her, Clinton's commitment to gender equality reflected God's priorities and therefore won Smith's support. "God created man and woman in his image, and gender inequality emerged post-Fall," Smith said. "So the movements of gender equality are works of God." Similarly Ellen Richard, a Bible editor at a Chicago-area Christian publisher, said, "I'm voting for Clinton because I'm committed to seeing women gain greater levels of power." Richard added that a Clinton presidency would balance what she considers to be "a historical wrong."[8]

When I heard these comments, I felt sad. I'm sure these Jesus feminists meant well and truly believed Clinton would improve the plight of women. But Clinton's brand of feminism, because it is rooted in anti-Christian beliefs and assumptions, ends up hurting women more than helping. The same could be said of third- and fourth-wave feminism too. The entire movement is rife with the same kind of misogyny manifested by Clinton herself over the past three decades.

She knew about her husband's alleged sexual abuse of women, yet instead of helping his victims, she reportedly spearheaded smear campaigns against them.[9] Clinton also displayed disdain for homemaking and motherhood, once quipping to reporters, "I suppose I could have stayed home and baked cookies and had teas, but what I decided to do was to fulfill my profession which I entered before my husband was in public life."[10] There's nothing wrong with pursuing a profession, but to characterize staying home full-time to be a mother as "baking cookies" and having "teas" showed an incredibly condescending view of stay-at-home motherhood.

Given Clinton's almost fanatical commitment to abortion, it's hard to imagine she valued motherhood at all. One of Clinton's biographers, Dr. Paul Kengor, a political science professor at Grove City College, once wrote, "[Abortion] is Hillary's hill to die on. I believe Hillary Clinton would give her life for *Roe v. Wade*."[11] It's hard to imagine why anyone would feel so passionately about retaining the right to kill her own progeny, but this is the ethic of today's feminism. Children and family are expendable; a woman's career is not.

Given her perverse values and malicious behavior, it's not surprising that Hillary Clinton was one of the most disliked presidential candidates in American history, which certainly contributed to her stunning loss to Donald Trump.[12] In the end Clinton failed to lock up the women's vote. A slight majority of women voted for her (54 percent),[13] but that was actually a smaller percentage than had voted for Obama just four years earlier (56 percent).[14] That Clinton failed to galvanize the female vote was even more surprising given some of the lewd and offensive comments her rival had made about women. Perhaps had her brand of feminism been more appealing, she could have rallied women to her side. But feminism, like the women who represent it, has become hollow and shrill. And though some Christian women today proudly embrace it, I suspect the majority of women believe we can do better. And we can.

FEMINISM'S SORDID PAST

Initially feminism aimed to abolish the misogyny that resulted from the Fall: man's domination and devaluation of woman. The aims of what is now called first-wave feminism were consistent with Christianity, and some Christians played a prominent role in it. This nineteenth- and early-twentieth-century movement addressed men's denigration of women—the refusal to grant women the right to vote, to own property (if married), and to pursue higher education and certain professions.[15] This feminism didn't seek its goals to the detriment of the family or women's roles as mothers. In fact, feminist pioneer Mary Wollstonecraft wrote in her famous work *A Vindication of the Rights of Women*, "The care of children in their infancy is one of the grand duties annexed to the female character by nature."[16]

Second-wave feminism, which began in the 1960s, radically departed from this original vision. Its ideological founder, Simone de Beauvoir, was an admirer of Karl Marx and Friedrich Engels, authors of *The Communist Manifesto*. As Dr. Paul Kengor (also an expert in Communism) documents in his book *Takedown: From Communists to Progressives; How the Left Has Sabotaged Family and Marriage*, both Marx and Engels wanted to abolish marriage. Engels specifically envisioned a communist society where the state would supplant the family, all housework would be nationalized, and mothers would be moved from homes to factories.[17]

This was utopia for Beauvoir, who believed the roles of wife and mother enslaved women. In her book, *The Second Sex*, she analyzes Friedrich Engels's book *The Origin of the Family*. "'Woman cannot be emancipated unless she takes part in production on a large social scale and is only incidentally bound to domestic work.' . . . Thus, woman's fate is intimately bound to the fate of socialism,"[18] she wrote. Beauvoir also wanted to abolish sexual differentiation. To her, equality required sameness. As long as man viewed woman as "other," he would seek to oppress her. Just as Marx and Engels advocated eradicating all economic and social classes, Beauvoir advocated eradicating all gender classes. In her ideal society there would "no longer be men or women, but only workers, equal among themselves."[19]

Given this radically antifamily and antigender stance, it is not surprising that Beauvoir, like Marx and Engels, was also a committed atheist. And just as Marx tied Communism to atheism ("Communism begins where atheism begins"),[20] so Beauvoir tied her feminism to atheism. "Among others, for Jews, Muslims, and Christians, man is the master by divine right: fear of God will stifle the slightest inclination of revolt in the oppressed."[21]

Beauvoir's anti-Christian ideas were picked up and popularized in the United States by Betty Friedan, the person normally credited with launching second-wave feminism. Friedan dedicated her hugely influential book, *The Feminist Mystique*, to Beauvoir, and like Beauvoir, Friedan harbored atheist and socialist sympathies. In the twenty-five years before the publication of her groundbreaking book, she worked as a "political activist" and "professional propagandist for the Communist left."[22] She also signed the Humanist Manifesto II, which called "traditional theism, especially faith in the prayer-hearing God" an "unproved and outmoded faith," and referred to "salvationism" as "harmful."[23] Like Beauvoir, Friedan portrayed housewives as prisoners and viewed femininity as a vice, not a virtue. She wrote, "Femininity . . . makes American women a target and a victim of the sexual sell."[24]

Friedan wanted a world free from any traditional sex roles and criticized her contemporary, anthropologist Margaret Mead, for not calling for their complete eradication. Mead, after studying various primitive cultures, asserted that most sex roles were not inherent but were the result of notions implanted early in children. Yet she couldn't escape the biological realities that differentiated men from women. In the end Mead still advised women to embrace motherhood and to "seek respect for their uniqueness as women." But Friedan rejected the concept that "anatomy is destiny" and despised encouraging women to "play the role of woman." She saw acknowledging sexual differences as furthering the "feminine mystique," which she believed kept women from achieving their full potential. Instead, she advocated for a world where "being a woman was no more and no less than being human."[25]

Friedan's brand of feminism quickly spread throughout the United States. In 1966 she cofounded the National Organization of Women (NOW). She also started an organization to push for abortion rights, which today is known as NARAL Pro-Choice America. And to give feminists a greater voice in politics, she and other leading feminists, such as Gloria Steinem and Bella Abzug, helped create the National Women's Political Caucus.[26]

FEMINISM IN THE CHURCH

Given the virulent anti-Christian basis of second-wave feminism, one would expect Christians to vehemently oppose it. And some did. But once Friedan's book was published, many Christian feminists took up her cause in the church. This began in more liberal, mainline Protestant churches, but by the 1970s the movement had spread to conservative evangelical churches. Like secular feminists, Christian egalitarians or "biblical feminists" advocated erasing gender differences too. As feminist critic Mary Kassian wrote, "Biblical feminists dealt with the problems they perceived in the church in essentially the same manner as secular feminists dealt with the problems in society. Both sought to obliterate sex roles and express equality through role interchangeability."[27]

These early biblical feminists appropriated as their *crux interpretum*, or foundation for interpreting all of Scripture, Galatians 3:28, which says "there is no male and female." The context of this passage makes it clear that the author is not calling for the obliteration of gender or sex roles, but merely asserting that both sexes have equal access to salvation in Christ Jesus. Yet egalitarians dubbed the verse "'the Magna Carta' of humanity" and made it their centerpiece.[28]

In a 1974 book cited by *Christianity Today* as one of the top fifty books that have shaped evangelicals,[29] biblical feminists Letha Dawson Scanzoni and Nancy A. Hardesty wrote, "Equality and subordination are contradictions. . . . This pattern cannot indicate an egalitarian marriage. True egalitarianism must be characterized by what sociologists call 'role-interchangeability.'"[30] This same idea was forwarded sixteen years later by Mary Stewart Van Leeuwen, a former senior editor for *Christianity Today*, in her influential book *Gender and Grace*. Drawing heavily from the social sciences, Van Leeuwen attempted to prove that sex-based behavioral tendencies were the result of the Fall, and that Christians should seek to minimize or even eliminate sex roles. "There is nothing unbiblical about traditional family roles," Van Leeuwen wrote. "But neither is the traditional family the only (or always the best) way to organize such roles for marital health, adequate parenting and kingdom service."[31]

In 2007 sociologist Jack Balswick and his wife Judith, a family therapist, further explored role interchangeability in their book *The Family: A Christian Perspective on the Contemporary Home*. They asserted that scripturally, the mother is no more important to a child's well-being than a father. Therefore switching roles as primary nurturers doesn't present a problem and could actually be a benefit because it encourages men to invest more in child-rearing. Katelyn Beaty cites the Balswicks in her 2016 book, *A Woman's Place*, noting: "Tasks and roles long considered fixed in biology or spiritual design are being traded, shared, and handed off at increasing rates." Yet, rather than decry this practice, Beaty celebrates it, upholding it as a "new marriage model" that enables women to pursue careers and outside interests.[32]

Not only is this new model being promoted in books, it's also being promoted in Christian communities such as Wheaton College—not the secular, liberal school that my colleague Janet attended, but the evangelical flagship in Wheaton, Illinois, where I am an alumna. A Wheaton student told me about a conversation in which one of her professors, similar to the Balswicks, suggested that the roles of mother and father are interchangeable. Men and women are just not that different, the professor said. Neither has something unique to give that the other could not just as easily give. And surprisingly, this student said all of her classmates participating in the discussion agreed with the professor's statement.

Another Wheaton student told me about a similar experience he had in an anthropology class involving a different female professor. This professor, who proudly expressed that she and her husband share equally in the raising of their children, stated that there is no inherent reason why mothers should serve as the primary caregivers of children. The student challenged this professor, noting that only mothers can nurse children. The professor was undeterred and expounded on the joys of modern technology, which allow mothers to express milk and be freed from the demands of motherhood. This kind of freedom, she asserted, is essential for women because in cultures where the burden of childcare has fallen on women, women have been unable to contribute significantly to society.[33] Apparently to this professor, motherhood is insignificant.

These attitudes are incredibly misogynistic, and they show that the perverse desire to imitate men described in the previous chapter is not confined to secularists but is rampant among Christians. Women used to glory in their uniquely feminine role as mothers. But now, spurred by biblical feminists, even Christian women are joining the chorus of our misogynistic society, devaluing motherhood and pursuing roles more admired and respected by culture. It's not just in the home and marketplace that Christian women are forsaking traditional roles and trading places with men. They're also exchanging roles in the church, spurred again by biblical feminists.

According to a poll by the Barna Group, the number of women pastors in Protestant church leadership doubled from 1999 to 2009.[34] About 24 percent of mainline Protestant congregations are now pastored by women, and 9 percent of evangelical congregations.[35] In her 1987 book, *Equal to Serve*, Gretchen Gaebelein Hull likened gender-specific roles in the church to segregation. Sounding like a Christian version of Betty Friedan, she declared, "The Bible does not teach that biology is destiny. Men and women are not interchangeable as males and females, but they are interchangeable as new creatures in Christ." She then urged the Christian community to be "sex blind" when assessing a person's qualifications for ministry. "We reverently affirm that our great God is an Equal Opportunity Employer. Can His church be less?"[36]

This embrace of second-wave feminism hasn't liberated women in the church. It's simply enabled the church to exhibit two forms of misogyny. In the complementarian church, misogyny assumes the form that prompted first-wave feminism—men failing to see women as complete persons and denying their gifting. In the egalitarian church, it exists in the same covert ways as in second-wave feminism—by denying that women possess anything special and encouraging them to exchange places with men. Instead of erasing misogyny in the church, egalitarianism simply found a new way to express it. Egalitarianism and complementarianism, then, are often just two sides of the same misogynistic coin. Both devalue women, and what is lost as a result is a flourishing and robust feminine presence in our homes and churches. Second-wave feminism did not help women; it simply diminished, or in some cases erased, femininity.

FEMINISM'S THIRD WAVE AND HOOKUP CULTURE

In the 1990s a third wave of feminism emerged that the church never embraced because it was so blatantly immoral. Yet its attitudes have certainly impacted Christians and likely contributed to the sexual practices common among teenage and young-adult Christians. Unlike second-wave feminists, who opposed pornography because they viewed it as degrading to women and furthering a culture of male domination, third-wave feminists embraced pornography and sexual license. Heavily influenced by the message of the sexual revolution, these daughters of second-wave feminists considered the porn-averse feminism of their mothers to be repressive. They believed sexual freedom was essential to women's freedom and, as a result, opposed any efforts to control or limit sexual activity. This "sex-positive" or "porn-positive" feminism embraced an entire range of new and alternative sexualities including gay, lesbian, bisexual, transsexual, transgendered, and queer. It also embraced and promoted the hookup culture, which is rampant among teenagers and young adults today.[37]

The results of third-wave feminism have been devastating to women. Traditional dating has become almost extinct, at least in secular settings, and has been replaced by casual sexual "hookups." Instead of dating leading to a serious relationship and then marriage and then sex, casual sex now regularly precedes relationship. These hookups may lead to a relationship, but they generally don't and can cause serious emotional and physical damage, especially for women. Yet women participate in this risky and degrading practice because feminists have told them it will make them happy. Moreover, hooking up has become for many women the only way to get a man. David Buss, a psychology professor at the University of Texas–Austin who specializes in human sexuality, said the hookup culture has made sex and women much more available to men. Since men don't have to make women a priority, they don't. And "women are forced to go along with [the hookup culture] in order to mate at all."[38]

On American college campuses, hookups are especially prevalent. Paula England, a sociologist at Stanford University, surveyed more than fourteen thousand college students at nineteen universities about their hookup and dating experiences from 2005 to 2010. She found that 72 percent of college coeds reported having at least one hookup by their senior year. But a sizable number of this group, 40 percent, had between four and nine hookups, and about 20 percent said they had ten or more.[39] Since 2010, however, the hookup culture has exploded due to dating apps such as Tinder and Hinge. One study reported that nearly one hundred million people now are using dating apps, some simply as a portal to shop for sex partners twenty-four hours a day. The results are chilling.[40]

Alex, a twentysomething investment banker, told a reporter for *Vanity Fair* that dating apps enable men like him to "rack up 100 girls [they've] slept with in a year." He said he had slept with five different women in the past eight days and couldn't recall all of their names. Alex's friend Marty said he had slept with thirty to forty women in the past year, but admitted he had to feign wanting a relationship to get them to have sex with him. "I think to an extent it is, like, sinister," he admitted and then mused, "Do you think this culture is misogynistic?"[41]

Of course it is—and it's alarming that women would participate in their own victimization on such a vast scale. But that is the nature of movements rooted in assumptions contrary to God's design. They promise fulfillment but deliver pain and bondage. Fallon, a female student at Boston College, told the *Vanity Fair* reporter, "Sex should stem from emotional intimacy, and it's the opposite with us right now, and I think it really is kind of destroying females' self-images." A classmate, Amanda, added, "But if you say any of this out loud, it's like you're weak, you're not independent, you somehow missed the whole memo about third-wave feminism."[42]

God designed women to bond emotionally with their sex partners, and engaging in casual sex violates that design. As doctors Joe S. McIlhaney Jr. and Freda McKissic Bush explain in *Hooked: New Science on How Casual Sex Is Affecting Our Children*, women's brains release oxytocin when they have sexual contact, causing them to bond with their partners whether they intend to or not. It's not surprising, then, that one study of nearly five hundred female college students found that women who casually engage in sex feel depressed afterward and have "poor mental health."[43] Equally devastating is what can happen to these women if they persist in this damaging activity. Over time their brains mold so that they no longer can bond with their sexual partners. McIlhaney and Bush wrote, "Their ability to bond after multiple liaisons is almost like tape that loses its stickiness after being applied and removed multiple times." (Men who engage in casual sex experience similar neurological changes, the authors explain, though a different chemical, called vasopressin, is involved.)[44]

Hookup culture is not only damaging emotionally; it's also physically dangerous. According to a 2015 report by the Centers for Disease Control and Prevention, sexually transmitted diseases (STDs) have hit an all-time high in the United States. Cases of syphilis were up 19 percent from 2014 to 2015, gonorrhea was up 12.8 percent, and chlamydia was up 5.9 percent. The increase in STDs has hit women especially hard. Chlamydia, for example, can damage a woman's reproductive system, but in most men the bacterial disease never produces any symptoms at all. Similarly, syphilis in pregnant mothers can be transmitted to their babies. Women's rate of syphilis diagnoses increased more than 27 percent from 2014 to 2015, and cases of congenital syphilis increased 6 percent over the same time period.[45]

Despite its ravaging impact, the hookup culture continues unabated, in part because many feminists see it as essential for fulfilling the priorities of second-wave feminism: career first and love, marriage, and family later, if at all. As Hanna Rosin, author of *The End of Men and the Rise of Women*, wrote, "Feminist progress right now largely depends on the existence of hookup culture. . . . For college girls these days, an overly serious suitor fills the same role an accidental pregnancy did in the nineteenth century: a danger to be avoided at all costs, lest it get in the way of a promising future."[46] No feminist dares to entertain the notion that these priorities may violate our basic nature or that pursuing them leads to our own demise. But that's precisely what this social experiment is proving to be true. Yet instead of scrapping feminism, feminists keep trying to morph and salvage it.

FEMINISM'S FOURTH WAVE AND THE ELIMINATION OF THE "GENDER BINARY"

In the past ten years, a fourth wave of feminism has begun to emerge, though it is so amorphous that even many leading feminists have trouble defining it. However, two characteristics stand out. One is that fourth-wave feminists are tech savvy. Instead of producing magazines and marching in protests, these young feminists are more likely to create blogs and online communities and to launch Twitter campaigns. These feminists also have a more global perspective because the Internet has exposed them to women's needs in other countries. So a fourth-wave feminist is often as concerned about human trafficking and women's access to education, contraception, and abortion in the developing world as she is about similar issues in the developed world.

Second, as noted earlier, fourth-wave feminists stress intersectionality—the theory that social identities and systems of oppression interact on many different levels. Essentially fourth-wave feminism results when feminism meets identity politics. Identity politics asserts that one's identity is largely defined by race, class, or gender/sexuality—and that one's politics is largely shaped by membership in one of these groups. What's new is seeing how the forces that allegedly oppress women may also interact or overlap with the forces that oppress other groups, such as racial minorities or those who identify as LGBTQ. A fourth-wave feminist feels a special affinity with other groups perceived as oppressed or marginalized, so she would be as likely to advocate for transgender bathrooms as she would for wage equality.

Certainly there are some causes that fourth-wave feminists and Christians have in common, such as fighting human trafficking or racial discrimination. But like second- and third-wave feminism, fourth-wave feminism is based on certain assumptions and beliefs that are decidedly anti-Christian. Scripture teaches that our identities, for example, are not fundamentally rooted in race, class, or gender/sexuality, but in our relationship to Christ.[47] Similarly our politics should not primarily be informed by race, class, or gender, but by our commitment to Christ and His kingdom.

Feminism's embrace of postmodern definitions of identity and political struggle may eventually lead to its complete undoing. After all, one of the major tenets of the LGBTQ community is that gender is not a biological fact but a social construction, and that the so-called gender binary—the division of society into male and female—is oppressive and should be abolished.[48] In this new gender-spectrum world, it's hard to imagine how feminism—something that assumes a gender binary—would have any legitimacy. It seems feminism would eventually have to be abolished along with all the other relics of the "oppressive" gender-binary world.

The irony is that when society erases gender distinctions, it also erases common-sense protections of women and perpetuates the injustice and oppression of them. For example, in an effort to accommodate transgender men and women, some schools and businesses are now allowing people to use whichever bathroom or locker room fits their chosen gender identity. However, having a biological boy who identifies as a girl in a high school changing area can be quite traumatic for girls who haven't likewise decided that anatomy doesn't matter. These bathroom and locker room policies have also opened the door to abuse by predatory men and boys. Just the other day, my teenage daughter ran into a Target to go to the bathroom, forgetting about the department store's controversial transgender bathroom policy. When she got to the bathroom, she saw two snickering teenage boys enter ahead of her. She thought of complaining to management but then remembered the store allows customers to use whichever bathroom they want, regardless of their biological sex. She then looked for a single-toilet bathroom and couldn't find one, so she left the store and suffered through a very uncomfortable trip home. Our family shuddered to think what might have happened had she arrived at the bathroom a few seconds later or earlier and encountered the boys in a secluded restroom.

The incident reminded me of Kaeley Triller Haver, a rape survivor I interviewed on a radio program exploring the bathroom wars. She explained that for her and the millions of other women who are sex abuse survivors, encountering a man in a women's bathroom would trigger feelings of panic and terror, even if nothing happened. But assaults do happen in bathrooms and locker rooms. In 2016 the Liberty Counsel, a Christian legal ministry, posted a list of fifty documented cases in which a man assaulted, attacked, endangered, or harassed a girl or woman in a women's bathroom or locker room.[49] Nevertheless, government, school, and business leaders continue to ignore this obvious threat to women, thanks in part to fourth-wave feminists.

On a similar note, fourth-wave feminists have helped open the door to men competing in women's competitions. This has led to disastrous results. In June 2015 a transgender mixed martial arts (MMA) fighter, Fallon Fox, destroyed a female competitor. Fox, who was born male but underwent a sex-change operation, gave her opponent a concussion and broke her eye socket in a mere two minutes and seventeen seconds. In a post-fight interview, the brutalized opponent said, "I've fought a lot of women and have never felt the strength that I felt in a fight as I did that night. I can't answer whether it's because she was born a man or not . . . I can only say, I've never felt so overpowered ever in my life, and I am an abnormally strong female in my own right."[50]

Some would argue, myself included, that women have no business competing in MMA. But this is just the tip of the iceberg. In 2016 the International Olympic Committee (IOC) allowed Caster Semenya, a hyperandrogenic woman—someone with a masculinized body due to abnormally high levels of testosterone—to compete in the Olympics without suppressing her testosterone levels. In the past the IOC had recognized that high levels of testosterone gave hyperandrogenic women an unfair advantage,[51] but then came pressure from LBGTQ activists and certain fourth-wave feminists, such as Jos Truitt, executive director of the online community *Feministing*.

Truitt argued that placing a limit on testosterone amounted to "gender policing" by "gender essentialists"—those who believe that men and women are inherently different. And since Semenya is from South Africa, Truitt added that racism also contributed, applying the theory of intersectionality to make her case. "Take the widespread obsession with binary gender essentialism, combine racist ideas about the femininity of African women, and you've got a nice, intersectional method for using the Games to maintain power's favorite hierarchies," she wrote. "It's yet another way to say that superpower nations, and men, are superior and the global south, and women, are inferior—even at playing games."[52] The IOC eventually capitulated to this pressure, rescinded the testosterone limit, and Semenya easily won gold in the 800 meters in the 2016 Games.

The IOC also changed its rules regarding transgender athletes before the 2016 Games. Previously transgender athletes were required to undergo sex-reassignment surgery and to wait two years before competing. However the IOC eliminated the surgery requirement, so now transgender athletes with male anatomy may compete as women, provided their testosterone levels fall below a certain limit.[53] The same logic that was applied to hyperandrogenic athletes will certainly be applied to transgender ones, and the testosterone limit on them will eventually be eliminated too. This will destroy women's sports, and feminists should be up in arms. Instead, they're celebrating these changes as human rights victories.

A TRUE FEMINISM

Feminism is failing because it has a false vision of womanhood and a wrong strategy for ending the oppression of women. The entire movement is a classic example of the mess humans create when they bypass God's design and attempt to create their own. The solution to the problem of men dominating women is not to erase legitimate gender categories and create a plethora of new ones, to adopt the soul-destroying sexual practices of the most depraved men, or to eliminate the feminine in ourselves and then swap roles with our male counterparts. What's desperately needed now is a feminism that tenaciously upholds God's design for womanhood and resists the lies of culture and the corrosive effects of sin. We need a generation of women who cherish their femininity and embrace their unique place in the world. After all, we can't expect men to respect and honor the beauty of womanhood if we don't value it ourselves. Only when we do can we redeem what's been perverted and lost and "shine among them like stars" in a "warped and crooked generation."[54]

True feminism would embrace the essential God-designed differences between the sexes and uphold the natural family. And it would seek to restore motherhood in the eyes of the culture and the church, promoting it as an essential component of a flourishing society, as well as a high spiritual calling. It would encourage mothers to put their families first. And, instead of urging young mothers to stay in the workforce at whatever cost, it would seek to empower them so they can choose to stay at home. That said, true feminism would resist legalism and one-size-fits-all solutions. It would recognize the unique challenges each woman faces and would support her as she seeks to fulfill God's call on her life. This new feminism would again deem it socially acceptable for young girls to proudly proclaim that they desire to be mothers when they grow up. It would stop treating motherhood as a hobby or part-time job and would elevate it to a place of prominence and respect.

It also would reject the notion that fathers can substitute for mothers. Men can be wonderful fathers—and they certainly have strengths that women don't—but God has uniquely equipped mothers to nurture children. Besides the obvious presence of a womb and breasts, scientists are now discovering other ways that God has specially designed women for motherhood. Just as oxytocin bonds women to their sexual partners, it bonds them to their babies. When a mother holds her baby next to her skin and nurses, her brain is flooded with oxytocin, which produces a powerful bond between her and her baby and predisposes the mother to sacrifice for her child.[55] Men can never bond with a baby the way a mother who carries her child for nine months and then nurses him can. They also can never exhibit a loving and nurturing feminine presence the way a healthy woman can. When it comes to nurturing, women have a distinct advantage.

This is difficult to prove empirically. As my pastor's wife once wrote on her blog, "Defending the calling and person of mother as unique from father is like explaining the universe, a cosmos with sun and moon—both of which are necessary to sustaining life. Once we have to quantify, dissect, and chart mother love, we have already lost something so profound, I'm not sure where to begin."[56] It's worth noting that polls consistently find that nearly twice as many Americans say their mothers had the greatest influence on them growing up compared to their fathers.[57] Mothers possess an incredible capacity to love and impact the next generation. We need to embrace and celebrate that.

We also need to embrace and celebrate men's strengths. God made men to be providers and protectors. Some of this is self-evident: God made men physically stronger. Scripture also supports this notion. In Ephesians 5:25, the apostle Paul tells husbands to lay down their lives for their wives, not vice versa. Similarly, in 1 Peter 3:7, men are told to live with their wives "in an understanding way, showing honor to the woman as the weaker vessel." Also, in the Old Testament, men are the ones who go into battle, not women. The one exception is Deborah, a judge of Israel who instructed Barak to lead a battle against the Canaanites. Barak refused to go unless Deborah went with him, and as a result, God gave the glory for Israel's military success to a woman named Jael while Barak was shamed.[58]

Male leaders also need to rethink what it means for man to be the head of the woman as Christ is the head of the church. Does Christ lead His church by marginalizing half of it and ignoring the gifts He's given them? No, He gives Himself up for her. He nourishes her. He commissions her for the work of the kingdom. We need a feminism that invites women into full participation in the mission of the church. This doesn't mean men should relinquish their God-given places of leadership; it means male leaders must recognize the full range of women's gifting and steward those gifts with as much diligence and care as they would any other resource.

Not only do men need to value women, but women must also value men. The feminist claim that "a woman needs a man like a fish needs a bicycle"[59] is patently false. Women desperately need men just as men desperately need women. God created the sexes to be interdependent, so neither sex is dispensable. When either sex fails to recognize this fact, the family, the church, and society suffer. We are experiencing the effects of this today. One in four children under the age of eighteen are now being raised without a father, and of those children, 45 percent live below the poverty line.[60] Children from single-parent families are also more likely to misbehave, get sick, drop out of high school, be unemployed, and take their own lives.[61] Similarly, single mothers are more likely than married mothers to suffer from depression and chronic stress.[62] Despite what feminists say, the facts prove mothers need husbands, and children need both moms and dads.

We must embrace a feminism that recognizes these facts and rests solidly on God's definition of man, woman, and family. Without these as a foundation, feminism is destined to fail. But with these as a foundation, all of society will flourish.

SEVEN

GENDER CONSTRUCTION

AND CONFUSION

"We need to move beyond the gender binary," stated a self-identified transgender student at the public high school in suburban Chicago where my husband, Neal, taught for nearly thirty years. The comment capped an hour-long program where several students who identified as either gay or transgender shared their truly heartrending stories to garner support for the LGBTQ cause.

This particular student told of a home life that was horrific. Her father reportedly abused her mother, and as a result her mother drank excessively and spoke regularly about taking her own life. The student recalled one morning when her mother repeatedly screamed that she wanted to kill herself. Wanting to escape, the girl stood outside her house, longing for the screaming threats to stop. When they finally did, she pleaded with her mom, "Next time you want to scream about killing yourself, can you just wait until I leave the house?"

The girl was experiencing excruciating pain and said she no longer wanted to identify as a girl. She wrapped her chest daily with an ACE bandage to conceal her breasts and then requested that everyone call her by a boy's name. To identify her as a girl caused her profound emotional trauma. The student expressed deep gratitude to a teacher who complied with her request and regularly referred to her as a boy. She, and other students who identified as LGBTQ, held this teacher up as a role model for others to emulate.

Unconditional acceptance of students' self-constructed gender and sexuality was the only compassionate response for teachers and staff, according to this LGBTQ group of students. Compassion required rejecting a so-called gender binary society—a society with only two gender choices, male and female. This was oppressive to students who identify as LGBTQ, they said. Being "assigned" male or female required LGBTQ students to conform to categories that simply didn't fit, but the invention of new categories would open the door for unprecedented personal emancipation.

When my husband came home and relayed this girl's story to me, my heart broke. I can only imagine the pain she suffered as a result of growing up in such an abusive and dysfunctional home. I desperately wanted to help this girl, but I knew the help I would have offered would not have been welcome. I would have urged this girl to seek Jesus in her pain and to believe that God could rewrite her story. I would have gladly walked alongside her in that journey, encouraging her and pointing her to Christ. But this student was firm in her resolve to reject her God-given sex, and my husband's school maintained a pretty impenetrable firewall against anyone wanting to offer spiritual assistance to students. Still I felt a great deal of empathy for this teenage girl. No one should experience what she had in her home. And who knows what any one of us would do given the same set of circumstances?

I also connected personally with aspects of this student's story. Though I have never experienced gender dysphoria (the feeling that one's true gender identity is opposite of one's biological sex), I know what it's like to feel like a misfit as a girl. As I mentioned earlier, I never felt as if I lived up to the church's image of womanhood in my childhood and young-adult years. But I didn't really feel as if I lived up to culture's standard either.

I was a quintessential tomboy as child, which was less accepted then than it is now. I loved playing sports and was fiercely competitive. And though I enjoyed playing dolls and games with my two older sisters, they would often exclude me because I was the youngest and not always able to enter their level of play. In some ways, I became the brother that my brother, David, never had. He read books on basketball, baseball, and soccer and taught me to play with impeccable technique. If I failed to put one knee down when fielding a grounder or to form my wrist into a gooseneck after shooting a basketball, he'd rake me over the coals. I often came in crying to my mother, but within several minutes would return to play more.

Growing up, I always felt as if the boys had more fun. When my sisters, my brother, and I would play Tarzan, my sisters always wanted to be Jane. I wanted to be Tarzan. (Who wants to play house when you could swing on vines and subdue wild beasts?) Instead of signing up for dance classes or crafts, I played Little League and became the first girl in our rural Pennsylvania county to advance to Pony League. I was the only girl in my home who learned to play Ping-Pong and chess, and I reveled in competing against my dad and brother. I also enjoyed pranking and getting into mischief. I wasn't a rebellious child, but I was a boisterous free spirit and perhaps more full of "snips and snails and puppy-dogs' tails" than "sugar and spice and everything nice."

To their credit—and to my emotional well-being—my parents never made me feel odd or communicated that there was anything wrong with my penchant for boyish endeavors. I could tell my mother actually cherished this quality in me and saw it as something we both shared. Though she never played sports with the boys, she played basketball in college. She sometimes recounted how when she was a child and living on the campus of Houghton College, she enjoyed capturing garter snakes and chasing college girls around with them. My grandpa would often remark with a twinkle in his eye that of all my mother's children, I was the one who reminded him most of her.

Still I struggled with my seemingly insufficient feminine identity. Once, when our family was on a missions trip in Africa, my brother convinced some of the missionaries and Africans that I was his little brother and my name was Ted. The incident humiliated me and earned a strong reprimand for my brother from my parents. But the nickname stuck, and throughout my childhood my brother called me Ted and instructed his friends to do the same. I also noticed as I grew up that other adults didn't share my parents' approval of my boisterous nature. I never fit in at Pioneer Girls, a Christian equivalent of Girl Scouts. I remember a leader once calling me "rowdy" in a derisive manner. Though I didn't know what the word meant, I immediately perceived that this woman disapproved of my personality. Boys sometimes gave me a hard time too. Though some admired me for going toe-to-toe with them, others clearly felt embarrassed when I bested them in competition, and they would respond cruelly. It also didn't help that my next oldest sister was extremely popular and attractive. When she would show up at my baseball games, the guys on the team would say things like, "Wow, why don't you look like her?"

During puberty I often felt inadequate and wondered if there was something wrong with me. I'll never forget when I was about thirteen and my father came to pick me up after a coed soccer game. When I came off the field, he proudly reported that everyone on the sidelines had said that I played just like one of the boys. I burst into tears. My poor father was completely flustered and tried in vain to convince me that he was proud of the way I played. What he didn't realize was that as an emerging woman, I longed for my dad to affirm my femininity, not my athleticism.

I often wonder what would have happened to me had it not been for my sisters and my mother. When I would display overly boyish mannerisms, they'd gently rebuke me. When we would go clothes shopping, they would veto my sporty and boyish selections and suggest something pretty and feminine instead. I remember putting on the feminine clothes they would select for me and feeling as if they just didn't fit who I was, but my sisters and mom would insist. I was interested enough in pleasing them and attracting the attention of boys that I would comply. Over time the clothes that had felt so out of place on my body began to feel normal as I increasingly embraced my feminine identity and received affirmation from others.

Today many would discourage this kind of intentional gender identity formation. Rather than being a God-created ideal to which we should conform, gender is seen as a social construct, which is no more fixed and essential than being right- or left-handed. So when an adolescent girl expresses that remaining female feels unnatural or oppressive, those around her encourage her to follow the inner compass of her heart. She is encouraged to conform her biology to match her feelings, not attempt to conform her feelings to fit her God-given biology. If this same girl expresses sexual attractions—whether to the same sex, opposite sex, or both—she is encouraged to embrace those attractions uncritically. She is told that to be authentic, she must follow her heart, regardless of what God, the church, or anyone else says.

A CLASH OF WORLDVIEWS

How people view sex and gender depends largely on their worldviews. Christian apologist Nancy Pearcey describes *worldview* as "an internal map that guides us in navigating reality." Every worldview, Pearcey says, has a fixed reference point or "ultimate explainer"—a true north to which everything else on the map is oriented. For the Christian, this ultimate explainer is God. Truth, then, is transcendent and outside of oneself. It is objective. God is truth,[1] regardless of what anyone thinks or feels.[2]

All other worldviews, however, replace God with something He created (an idol) as their fixed reference point. This is the kind of idolatry the apostle Paul described in Romans 1:22–23. "Claiming to be wise," he wrote, "they became fools, and exchanged the glory of the immortal God for images resembling mortal man and birds and animals and creeping things." These idols give a false view of reality, causing us to believe lies and make bad decisions.

Since a Christian worldview is founded on God as truth, it reveals an accurate picture of the nature of humankind and of human gender and sexuality. God created man and woman as two inherently different persons. He established marriage as the union of one man and one woman for the purpose of revealing the nature of our triune God and the relationship between Christ and His church. Sex in any other context perverts this deeply spiritual and profound meaning of sex and marriage. Masculinity and femininity are not merely social constructions. They are characteristics of God, reflected in His creation and embodied uniquely, though not uniformly, in men and women.

The prevailing notions of gender and sexuality in our culture, in contrast, are based on a postmodern worldview in which the ultimate explainer is the community. "Postmodernism absolutizes the forces of culture or community," Pearcey wrote. "Truth has been redefined as a social construction, so that every community has its own view of truth, based on its experience and perspective, which cannot be judged by anyone outside the community."[3] One postmodern theologian, Stanley Grenz, put it this way: "There is no absolute truth: rather truth is relative to the community in which we participate."[4] Or as postmodern philosopher Richard Rorty put it, truth is merely "intersubjective agreement" among participants in a particular community.[5]

Not surprisingly, then, our postmodern culture views gender and sexuality as something each person constructs. Our culture rejects the created order of male and female—the "gender binary"—as simplistic and oppressive, and it replaces it with the "gender spectrum," the belief that "gender occurs across a continuum of possibilities."[6] So what began in the mid-1980s as LGB (lesbian, gay, bisexual) has now evolved to LGBTQQIP2SAA, which stands for Lesbian, Gay, Bisexual, Transgender, Queer (an umbrella term that includes all gender and sexual minorities), Questioning (those exploring their sexuality), Intersex (people whose anatomy or chromosomal makeup doesn't fully correspond to male or female), Pansexual (can be attracted to members of all gender identities and biological sexes), 2S (a term some indigenous peoples use to describe their gender, sexual, or spiritual identity), Asexual (does not experience sexual attraction), and Allies (does not identify as LGBTQ, but supports those who do).[7] But even this expansive acronym allegedly excludes many genders because no two people are alike. Theoretically, the number of genders could be as numerous as the population.

In the fall of 2016, my husband received a tutorial on this gender spectrum at a training event for teachers at his school. A school social worker distributed and explained a diagram of the Genderbread Person, a "tasty little guide" designed to help people better understand gender (see appendix). The diagram identified four gender/sexual categories corresponding to different parts on the Genderbread Person:

1. sexual attraction (the heart),
2. biological sex (the genitals),
3. gender expression (the exterior—dress and actions), and
4. gender identity (the brain).

Within each of these categories were two lines, or continua, corresponding in some way to the binary of male/female, masculine/feminine, or man-ness/woman-ness.

The handout instructed participants to plot a point along each line in each category indicating the extent to which they align with the characteristic each line represented. Taken together, these plot combinations represented each person's unique and personalized gender. Someone who aligned just slightly more along the man-ness continuum than he did along the woman-ness continuum might identify as gender-queer. Or a person who expressed herself as more masculine than feminine might be labeled "butch." The graphic noted that the "possible plot and label combinations" are infinite, which, if one accepts the diagram, is true because every line has infinite points.

What struck me about this diagram was its complete lack of sources. It seemed to me that if people were going to base their identities on something, it should at least have some concrete validation. I visited the website printed on the diagram and downloaded the book that explains the diagram in more detail. The book was nearly void of sources too. Yes, there was a bibliography at the back, but generally the author, Sam Killermann, asserted his ideas without grounding them in anything objective. At one point, he even admitted that his system of gender identification could be unreliable: "Defining and labeling specific gender identities creates a system of understanding that's as reliable as the hyperdrive on the Millennium Falcon. That is, relying too heavily on them often leads to more bad than good, but when they work they can make the Kessel Run in less than 12 parsecs."[8] This is classic postmodernism. Essentially what Killermann is saying is that this "truth" may be a fiction, but it works for the community most of the time, so let's embrace it.

Killermann's description of how he created the Genderbread Person is enlightening too. He said he began constructing it according to "the best available gender schema." Gender schema refers to the theory that children learn what it means to be male and female from the society in which they live. Through their experiences, they form schema, or models, about how men and women should behave, and then these schemas inform how they think and process their world.[9] Essentially the author based his Genderbread Person on gender theory that begins with an unproven premise: gender is not essential but socially constructed.

After publishing the first version of the Genderbread Person, Killermann said he received hundreds of e-mails complaining that his graphic wasn't inclusive of all genders. So he did what any good postmodern would do. He interviewed hundreds of people, "ranging the gamut of gender identities." Then he synthesized everything he heard, and with the help of a comprehensive sex educator, developed his own new and improved gender schema—the Genderbread Person 2.0. And then 3.3.[10] The Genderbread Person is a classic example of postmodern "truth." By its author's own admission, it is an "intersubjective agreement"—merely the synthesis of hundreds of people's subjective experiences.

To be fair, I should note that Killermann does cite two sources that could be regarded as objective. One is the research of Alfred Kinsey, which according to Killermann, shows that "most people aren't 100 percent straight or gay" but exist somewhere on a continuum. In citing Kinsey, Killermann is not unique. In fact, Kinsey, whose landmark studies of sexual behavior helped usher in the sexual revolution, is considered one of the most influential Americans of the twentieth century. However, using Kinsey's sex research as a measure of normative sexual behavior is like going to a *Star Trek* convention and concluding that the majority of Americans are highly intelligent but have the social skills of a preteen.

Kinsey's research is completely unreliable because he used severely skewed research samples. They included fourteen hundred imprisoned sex offenders, several hundred male prostitutes, and adults who were sexually abused as children. About 75 percent of his adult male subjects volunteered to give their sexual histories, and Stanford University researchers have found that volunteers for sex studies are two to four times more sexually active than those who don't volunteer.[11] The only thing Kinsey's research reveals is the sexual habits of a fringe population.

The other possibly objective source Killermann cites are statistics concerning the frequency of intersex births. Killermann argues that these statistics show humans are not born biologically male or female but exist along a continuum. Here again Killermann is not unique. Almost every LGBTQ group and website mentions intersex persons as evidence of the gender spectrum. In fact, the Gender Spectrum website asserts that "biological gender occurs across a continuum of possibilities. . . . This spectrum of anatomical variations by itself should be enough to disregard the simplistic notions of a binary gender system."[12]

According to the statistics Killermann cites, as many as one in every one hundred births, or 1 percent of the human population, are born with bodies that "differ from standard male and female." These numbers are hugely inflated, based on research done by Anne Fausto-Sterling of Brown University, because they include people most clinicians do not consider to be intersex, such as those with Klinefelter's syndrome and Turner syndrome.[13]

Those with Klinefelter's syndrome, for example, are clearly men but have an additional X chromosome. Similarly, those with Turner syndrome are clearly women but lack two complete X chromosomes. In both cases, their chromosomal sex matches their phenotypic (or physically visible) sex. According to an article published in the *Journal of Sex Research*, the term *intersex* "should be restricted to those conditions in which chromosomal sex is inconsistent with phenotypic sex, or in which the phenotype is not classifiable as either male or female." Using this more precise definition, the actual prevalence of intersex is about .018 percent—less than two one-hundredths of a percent. In other words, more than 99.98 percent of humans are born biologically male or female.[14]

Overall the Genderbread Person and the gender spectrum are based on bad reporting, faux science, and mere conjecture. Yet our culture, which is increasingly postmodern, has come to accept this false narrative. And more and more, the church is accepting it too. We are ceasing to think as Christians. We are, as Ephesians 4:14 describes, "infants, tossed back and forth by the waves, and blown here and there by every wind of teaching and by the cunning and craftiness of people in their deceitful scheming" (NIV).

SEXUAL AND GENDER CONFUSION IN THE CHURCH

For about two thousand years, the church enjoyed consensus on issues of gender and sexuality. It unanimously upheld marriage as the union of one man and one woman, and it forbade sexual relations in any other context. Today, however, that consensus no longer holds, and the church seems as confused about gender and sexuality as the world is. According to a 2015 Pew Research Study, 54 percent of American Christians see no conflict between homosexuality and their religious beliefs. Even among the most conservative Christians—white evangelical Protestants and black Protestants—25 percent and 43 percent respectively embrace a gay-affirming stance.[15]

Christians are also becoming more accepting of transgenderism. In 2015 the Reverend Duncan Dormor, dean of chapel and director of studies for theology at St. John's College, University of Cambridge, gathered and assessed the official positions on sexuality and gender for as many denominations as possible. He discovered that over the past several years, attitudes have been shifting and "there is growing momentum for change; for acceptance and welcoming of transgender Christians," especially within Protestant denominations.[16] In the Church of England, for example, Reverend Dormor found there were at least eight transgender priests serving within the church. The church also adopted a Gender Recognition Act in 2004 that specifically granted transsexual parishioners permission to use their parish church. In the United States, the Presbyterian Church USA voted in 2010 to allow ordination of transgender clergy, and in 2012, the Episcopal Church followed suit.[17]

What is happening in the church today is simply idolatry. Though we profess Christ, we are following a postmodern map of reality that has exchanged God—the unchanging, objective truth—for the subjective truth of the LGBTQ community. Instead of relying on what Scripture tells us about sex and gender, we rely on the definitions of sex and gender asserted by postmodern culture. Every LGBTQ-affirming Christian I have encountered starts with LGBTQ identity as given. Whatever the argument—whether it's asserting that the Bible's prohibitions on homosexuality no longer apply, or that celibacy is unreasonable and cruel—the premise is always the same: LGBTQ identity, the belief that same-sex attraction is innate and immutable, is a fact.

Matthew Vines, author of *God and the Gay Christian*, offers a prime example of this when discussing Romans 1:26–27 which says:

> Because of this [exchanging the truth of God for a lie—idolatry], God gave them over to shameful lusts. Even their women exchanged natural sexual relations for unnatural ones. In the same way the men also abandoned natural relations with women and were inflamed with lust for one another. Men committed shameful acts with other men, and received in themselves the due penalty for their error.

The passage seems pretty straightforward. However, Vines says the fact that the apostle Paul stated that women and men exchanged opposite-sex relations for same-sex relations betrays Paul's belief that these people were *"capable* of heterosexual attraction." Vines asserts that this understanding is false. "As the failure of the modern 'ex-gay' movement has shown . . . that isn't the case for gay people," he wrote. "Gay people cannot choose to follow opposite-sex attractions because they have no opposite-sex attractions to follow—nor can they manufacture them."[18]

This is a huge assertion. Vines is saying that innate, unchangeable gay identity is fact, and that this fact escaped the apostle Paul. Note that the starting point for Vines is not what Scripture says about identity; it's what culture and the failure of the ex-gay movement say about identity. Of course, there are a myriad of possible explanations for the collapse of the ex-gay movement besides Vines's assumption that gay people can't develop same-sex attractions. Perhaps chief among them was the unbiblical leadership of Alan Chambers, who served as president of the largest ex-gay ministry, Exodus International, from 2001 until its collapse in 2013.

In the years leading up to Exodus's collapse, Chambers succumbed to the heresy of antinomianism. This is the belief that because Christians are saved by grace, they have no obligation to keep God's moral law.[19] Not surprisingly, Chambers began openly affirming same-sex relationships shortly after Exodus folded and even marched in the Capital Pride Parade.[20] The collapse of Exodus received national media attention, giving the impression that the ex-gay movement had died. However, dozens of ex-gay ministries remain, ones that don't promise to convert gay people to being straight but instead offer healing to sexually broken people and hope for change. Many of these ministries are members of the Restored Hope Network, which is led by Ann Paulk, a godly and compassionate woman who has experienced change in her sexual orientation.[21]

Ann is not unique. There are hundreds of ex-gay people around the world who testify that they have experienced change in their sexual attractions. Supporting their testimonies is a study by Drs. Stanton Jones and Mark Yarhouse, showing that change is possible for some. Their seven-year study of ninety-eight individuals trying to change their same-sex orientation showed that 23 percent experienced successful conversion to heterosexual orientation; 30 percent said they were able to live chastely and no longer identified with same-sex orientation; 27 percent continued the process of attempted change with limited and unsatisfactory success; and only 20 percent gave up and fully embraced gay identity. Surprisingly the attempt to change did not normally lead to increased psychological distress but actually decreased distress in some.[22]

Vines's assertion is unfounded, but since it supports the accepted intersubjective agreement of our culture, it is the "truth" many professing Christians accept and to which they require Scripture to conform. Vines acknowledges this tendency. He wrote, "So, some might ask, does that mean Paul was wrong and the Bible is in error?"[23] In other words, does our postmodern truth show God's revealed truth to be wrong? This is where many LGBTQ-affirming Christians land. When the Bible and postmodern "truth" collide, they simply declare that the Bible is outdated and needs revision. The United Church of Christ, one of the first mainline denominations to affirm same-sex relationships, does this. The church asserts that the Bible is not "frozen in time," but evolves with each generation because we serve a "still-speaking God."[24] However, Vines is from a conservative Christian background and seeks to convert other conservative Christians who view God's Word as unchanging and authoritative. So he's developed a rhetorical work-around.

According to Vines, people in Paul's time didn't view homosexuality as we do today. They didn't have the categories of LGBTQ, so those who participated in homosexual behavior were not seen as exclusively same-sex attracted. They were simply seen as people whose sexual appetites exceeded heterosexual activity. Also, people in the first century didn't conceive of homosexuality as something that might be expressed in a committed, loving relationship. Though these relationships existed, they were extremely rare. The most common same-sex behaviors in the Greco-Roman world involved pederasty, prostitution, and sex between masters and slaves. Given this cultural context, Vines concludes, "Paul wasn't condemning the expression of a same-sex orientation as opposed to the expression of an opposite-sex orientation. He was condemning *excess* as opposed to *moderation*."[25]

There is nothing in the biblical text to suggest this reinterpretation. And again Vines's interpretation assumes gay identity as fact— something Vines admits the biblical writers never even entertained in their imaginations. They couldn't have because gay identity is only 150 years old. Prior societies viewed and practiced homosexuality in a variety of ways, but none considered it a fixed trait of a fundamentally different kind of person.[26] In fact, influential postmodern philosopher Michel Foucault, who regularly engaged in homosexual activity, suggested that modern notions of sexuality were not discovered by nineteenth- and twentieth-century thinkers but were created. "Homosexuality appeared as one of the forms of sexuality," he said, "when it was transposed from the practice of sodomy onto a kind of interior androgyny, a hermaphrodism of the soul. The sodomite had been a temporary aberration; the homosexual was now a species."[27]

Scripture repeatedly refers to homosexuality as sin, not as an immutable trait. Not only is this clear in Romans 1, but Paul reiterates this view in 1 Corinthians 6:9–11. After stating that "men who practice homosexuality" will not inherit the kingdom of God, the apostle Paul says, "And such *were* some of you. But you were washed, you were sanctified, you were justified in the name of the Lord Jesus Christ" (emphasis added). To accept Vines's interpretation one must accept that today's proponents of gay identity are actually more enlightened than the writers of Scripture, that the LGBTQ community knows the truth about homosexuality while the authors of Scripture were woefully ignorant. This is not a high view of Scripture, as Vines claims. It is an astonishingly low view of Scripture that places biblical understanding below postmodern truth.

Vines's view also ignores the consistent and overarching view of sexuality and gender that's presented throughout the Bible. As we have discussed, marriage as the one-flesh union of husband and wife is the great metaphor of Scripture—the key to understanding who God is, who we are, and how God relates to His church.[28] And since this metaphor communicates profound spiritual mysteries, such as God's triune nature and the relationship of Christ to His church, distorting it in any way has serious consequences. God gave us these symbols because we need them to comprehend complex and mind-blowing transcendent realities. But if the symbol is perverted, then so is our ability to understand the Godhead and how we relate to Him.

If one substitutes two men or two women for the one man and one woman in the one-flesh union, then the entire symbol is perverted. It fails to show unity with distinction and instead reflects unity in sameness. It also fails to reflect the life-giving nature of Trinitarian love because unlike heterosexual union, homosexual union is always sterile. Same-sex unions, then, are essentially symbolic blasphemy. Instead of two people reflecting the truth about our Trinitarian God, they are reflecting a lie.

Same-sex marriage destroys the symbolic purpose of marriage as a reflection of Christ's relationship with His bride, the church. Christ, as the masculine bridegroom, initiates with us. He sacrifices for us and lays down His life for us. The church, as His feminine bride, responds. We receive His gift of salvation and live in a constant state of responding to His divine initiative. Here again, same-sex marriage destroys the truth God created marriage to reflect. Marriage between two men or two women does not convey the masculine initiative and feminine response inherent in Christ's relationship with the church. Instead it conveys all initiation (two men) or all response (two women) and again perverts the spiritual purpose for which God created the symbol of marriage.

In a recent discussion with an LGBTQ-affirming Christian, I explained this symbolic distortion. He responded by asking me what importance I place on experience. When I asked him why he asked the question, he said, "I just believe that [my transgender friend] is a woman." He then admitted that the difference between us was that

I saw Scripture as true and unchanging, but he viewed it as something that changes to match our experience. That was an astonishing admission—and as much as it grieves me to say it, it places this person in grave danger. In Revelation 22:18–19, God issues a sobering warning to anyone who would add or subtract anything from the Word of God: "God will add to him the plagues described in this book" and "will take away his share in the tree of life and in the holy city." God does not excuse idolatry. We must accept Him as our fixed and unchanging point of reference. Failing to do so will destroy not only our afterlives, but our lives on earth as well.

PURSUING A REVEALED IDENTITY, NOT A CONSTRUCTED ONE

Recently, I Googled the self-identified transgender student who spoke at my husband's school's Transgender Lunch-n-Learn. She now looks very much like a he. She has facial hair and is undergoing hormone therapy. She has had her breasts removed and is anticipating getting complete sex-change surgery as soon as she has the money. "I was just born in the wrong body," she said.

I felt so much sadness over this young woman's bodily transformation. I don't believe she was born in the wrong body. God doesn't make mistakes; we do. I don't know all the factors that caused this young woman to despise her femininity, but clearly her self-directed misogyny was intense. She said at one point that she hated her female body so much she attempted suicide. I couldn't help but wonder if observing her mother's abuse contributed to this woman's aversion to the feminine. I also wondered how things might have been different had she known Christ. What if she had been affirmed in her identity as a child of God and had truly experienced how much God loves her feminine body and her feminine soul? What if she had been encouraged to follow a Christian map of reality as opposed to a postmodern one?

Sadly, many who follow the paths of their own re-creations never find peace or self-acceptance. According to a 2003 Swedish study, life usually gets worse for those who undergo sex-change surgery. Many experience an increase in mental difficulties about ten years after surgery, and their suicide mortality rate ten to fifteen years after surgery is almost twenty times greater than the comparable nontransgender population.[29] Proverbs 14:12 says, "There is a way that appears to be right, / but in the end it leads to death" (NIV). This is the way of the world, and this is the destination to which every idolatrous map leads. Jesus pleads with us to walk the narrow way: "I am the way and the truth and the life."[30] "Enter through the narrow gate. For wide is the gate and broad is the road that leads to destruction."[31] The question facing Christians today is, will we follow Jesus or a god of our own making?

My family of origin was not perfect, but if I compiled every mistake my parents ever made, those would be nothing compared to the surpassing gift they gave me in pointing me to Christ. They taught me that Christ is the solid rock and everything else is shifting sand. And so, even in my deepest pain and confusion, I could always find true north. I had a reliable map that told me who I was, where I was going, and how I should act. Because of God's Word, I could always make course corrections. I could always find my way home.

EIGHT

REDEMPTIVE SUFFERING

"Right now, I just need to escape." I remember instant messaging those words to a friend when I was in the throes of my dysfunctional relationship with Sarah. I was in agony at the time. I didn't know what was happening to me or why; all I knew was I hurt like crazy and wanted it to stop.

"What kind of escape are we talking about?" my friend messaged back. "Because if you're talking about infidelity or something of that nature, I can't really support you. But, if you're talking about going out and getting a few drinks, I'm in."

So that night my friend and I went out to a bar. I can't remember what she drank, but I drank whiskey sours. I come from a family of teetotalers and had never really drunk before, so I had no idea what to order. I had once tasted a whiskey sour and liked it, so it became my drink of choice that night. Something about being at a bar and drinking felt rebellious to me, despite being thirteen years over the legal drinking age. When you grow up in a home like mine, it doesn't take much. And, for some reason, crossing over this imaginary boundary (I didn't even think drinking was wrong) enabled me to open up.

Until that night I hadn't told anyone about the inner turmoil I was experiencing. I was terrified of what conclusions people might draw. I was terrified to draw my own conclusions. I realize now that my codependency with Sarah was simply a broken response to deficits in my life. Once those deficits were addressed and healed, the dependency and strong emotions subsided. But that night, I was so confused and so distraught. Yet, in the safety of my friend's company, I shared everything—and it felt incredibly liberating. My friend didn't judge. She didn't try to solve my problem. She just listened. We talked for hours—not just about my pressing issue, but about our husbands, our families, and our childhoods.

We laughed about my incredibly sheltered upbringing. She didn't grow up in a Christian home and found my naïveté amusing. Over the course of our conversation, I happened to mention that I hadn't ever even smoked a cigarette. Something about smoking a pack of cigarettes fit the mood we were in. So we left the bar, bought a pack of cigarettes, and smoked them in my green Escort wagon while exchanging more stories.

Today I feel embarrassed about that night. We didn't get drunk—perhaps a bit tipsy—but I had acted like an immature teenager, despite being a thirty-four-year-old mother of two and a leader in the church. Even so, that night was cathartic for me. My anxiety had built to the point where I felt as if I was going to explode. But after spilling everything to my friend, I went home, slept like a baby and, for the next day or so, felt incredibly relieved.

Of course the anxiety returned, and for the first time in my life, I felt an overwhelming temptation to escape. Alcohol, weed, illicit relationships—it didn't matter the form. I just wanted relief. I had never experienced anything like that before. I had grown up relatively happy. Even when I had experienced depression in college, I had never seriously considered anesthetizing it with drugs or sex. But now the pull was incredibly strong.

Fortunately, I was naive. I had no idea how to get drugs, and I had a husband and two kids who were all strong incentives to avoid foolishness. And I loved Jesus. Even as a teenager, I remember feeling that I would hurt Jesus if I partied or crossed sexual boundaries with my boyfriends. That reluctance to hurt God helped me avoid those sins and served as a strong deterrent once I was an adult.

I also knew the escapes would be temporary. And the options I was entertaining were not innocuous, like my mildly rebellious night with my friend. They would cause damage—not just to my relationship with God, but to my relationships with my husband, my children, and myself. In some ways, my predicament reminded me of giving birth. I knew the only way out of the pain was through it. God had put me in this difficult circumstance, and I sensed that if I faced my pain, I could get to the bottom of whatever was happening to me. If I pressed in, if I allowed the Holy Spirit to work, if I didn't run but braved whatever would come, then Jesus would make me whole.

That one night was the extent of my escaping. Within a few weeks I was enrolled in the healing program my close friends had recommended. I really didn't know what I was getting into or what to expect. Every Wednesday night for nine months I drove thirty-five miles into Chicago and gathered with about three to four dozen other people similarly seeking healing. Participating in that ministry was a lot like Naaman having to dip seven times in the Jordan River.[1] Besides dredging up a lot of pain, it was humiliating to admit my brokenness and need, and to join a group of fellow strugglers. Part of me would have rather reverted to my college days of ducking into a bathroom to cry and then pretending to the world that everything was okay. But I was done with pretending and didn't want to run; I wanted to get better.

Our meetings typically began with thirty minutes of worship. Then we'd listen to a talk on topics ranging from "holy father love" and "the true self" to "family of origin," "masculine and feminine," and "codependency." The messages drew from Scripture but also from psychology and sources new to me—such as the church fathers. I was amazed at the depth and relevance of the material. Almost every talk connected to something in my history or current experience and took me deeper in my relationship with God. After each talk, I was usually eager to join my small group of six to eight women to process what I had heard and to receive prayer.

That season of healing was incredibly fruitful, but it was incredibly painful too. My emotions were extremely raw. And rather than calm them, our weekly meetings often agitated my fragile state. I cried so much during our small group that it became customary for our leaders to grab a roll of toilet paper before we began our ministry time. (For some reason, Kleenex was never available.) During this time I quickly learned why healing is the road less traveled. It requires facing wounds and deficits we would rather avoid. And it forces us to be vulnerable with other people, to drop our facades, and to admit how truly broken we are. I thank God that He gave me the hope and will necessary to travel that road, but I grieve that so few are willing to follow that same path. Though the first few miles are treacherous and difficult, the road eventually smooths and leads to a much better destination.

THE WALKING WOUNDED

During more than twenty-five years of ministry, I have observed that almost everyone needs healing of some sort. Sadly, only a fraction pursue it. Though both women and men suffer the tragic consequences of sin, we do not suffer equally or in the same way. Because of the Fall, the powerful prey on the weak. And despite attempts by many women in our culture to become strong and impenetrable, we are the weaker sex. We are disproportionately victims, and as a result, we need healing perhaps even more desperately than our male counterparts.

Though my primary wounding had nothing to do with being verbally, physically, or sexually assaulted, that is not the case for many women. Clinical psychologist Juli Slattery and her colleague, Linda Dillow, have ministered to thousands of women through their teaching ministry, Authentic Intimacy. Very rarely do they meet a woman who has not been scarred or wounded in her sexuality.[2] Sin is just so pervasive—and women are so vulnerable—that significant wounding of this kind is unavoidable for far too many.

According to the Centers for Disease Control, nearly one in five women has been raped at some point in her life. Add to that number those who have been victims of physical violence and stalking, and the proportion jumps to one in every three women.[3] Women abused in these ways suffer from serious emotional trauma. According to one study, 94 percent of rape victims experience symptoms of post-traumatic stress disorder (PTSD) during the two weeks after the rape.[4] Nine months later, about 30 percent still report these symptoms.[5] Many rape victims also suffer from depression. About a third of them report at least one period of major depression in their lives.[6]

Sadly, very few victims of physical or sexual assault get the help they need. A stunning 63 percent of sexual assaults are never reported to police.[7] Because sexual brokenness is so private, Slattery and Dillow say, "Women typically don't reach out for hope or help. Instead they limp along, assuming that their stories will never be rewritten."[8]

Many women, including Christian women, are also profoundly scarred by abortion—an epidemic in our society. Every year more than one million women have abortions in the United States. According to the Guttmacher Institute, about 20 percent of these women (about two hundred thousand a year) identify as either evangelical, charismatic, fundamentalist, or born-again Christian.[9] Though men have been known to suffer from depression, guilt, grief, and feelings of powerlessness after abortion, very few studies have documented how prevalent these reactions are.[10] But given that women carry the unborn baby inside their bodies and then undergo invasive and often traumatic procedures to kill that baby, it's not surprising that postabortive women suffer profoundly. A study published in the *Medical Science Monitor* found that 65 percent of the postabortive American women studied experienced symptoms of PTSD, which they attributed to their abortions.[11] Other studies show that women who have had abortions are more likely to be hospitalized for psychiatric treatment, to suffer from sleep disturbances, to suffer from depression and anxiety, to abuse alcohol and marijuana, and to exhibit suicidal behavior.[12] Yet these women often do not seek help either.

Over the past several years, I have interviewed dozens of Christian women in various areas of pro-life activism and ministry. Every one of them says that those who have actually confessed and dealt with their abortions are a small minority. The shame runs too deep—and the fear of rejection is too strong. Kathy Rutledge, who leads an abortion-recovery ministry at a nondenominational church in Kentucky, kept her abortion secret for years. In that time, her shame about her abortion kept her from volunteering at church and made her fear God's punishment. Struggling with these unrelenting thoughts and feelings, she eventually attended a healing retreat for postabortive women and experienced God's forgiveness in a way she had never thought possible. Now Rutledge sometimes speaks about abortion at other churches. Unfortunately, she said many postabortive women want to avoid the subject—and so do many church leaders.

Rutledge said she once gave her testimony to a group of women at a megachurch in the South. By the end, several women were practically bawling, she said. Yet, when Rutledge asked the leaders about doing a follow-up, they said, "None of my women have had an abortion . . . and even if they did, they don't need to be speaking about it."

"These women have no idea how this is affecting every facet of their lives—their relationships with their husbands, their children," Rutledge told me. Another postabortive woman I interviewed agreed. She likened women's silence about their abortions to a splinter in the flesh. "Until you get it out," she said, "the healing really can't begin. It just continues to fester."[13]

Given the prevalence and seriousness of wounding among women, it's no wonder that so many are suffering from an assortment of addictions and patterns of sin. Pornography addiction, once thought to be only a man's problem, now reportedly affects 20 percent of Christian women.[14] Similarly, infidelity, which once was far more prevalent among men, is now almost equally prevalent among women.[15] A study published by the National Opinion Research Center found that over the past two decades, the percentage of wives who have admitted affairs has risen almost 40 percent.[16] Women also are succumbing to gambling more than they used to. Among gamblers aged forty-five to sixty-four, women now outnumber men.[17] Alcoholism used to affect mainly men, but now about a third of alcohol dependents or alcohol abusers in the United States are women—a whopping 4.6 million.[18]

Women also are battling traditional female vices, such as eating disorders. According to the National Eating Disorders Association, about twenty million American women will suffer from a "clinically significant eating disorder" sometime in their lives.[19] Women also disproportionately engage in self-injury, such as cutting or burning.

Some estimate that as many as two million people in the United States engage in this harmful behavior.[20]

Though I am sure there are multiple factors contributing to these problems in women, certainly some, if not most, stem from deep unresolved pain and wounding. Clearly, our methods of escape and pain avoidance are not working. These dysfunctional methods are similar to trying to hold an inflated beach ball underwater. Try as we may, that beach ball is going to find its way to the surface—and attempting to hold it under water indefinitely is pointless.

REDEMPTIVE SUFFERING

In his book *Wounds That Heal*, former pastor and Asbury Theological Seminary professor Dr. Stephen Seamands compares the process of healing to breaking the sound barrier. When pilots first attempted this feat, they found they had to steer their planes into a nosedive to achieve the required speed. As they would cross the sound barrier, shock waves and a sonic boom would throw them into a tailspin. When this would happen, pilots would instinctively pull back on the center stick and reduce their speed in an effort to gain control. These efforts proved unsuccessful, and the early pilots plunged to their deaths.

The first person to break the sound barrier and live did so by doing something radical and counterintuitive. Instead of trying to slow his plane down after breaking through the sound barrier, he accelerated it. This counteracted the effects of the shock waves and sonic boom, allowing the pilot to bring his plane out of the dive and under control. The same is true in healing, Seamands wrote. "The way to healing is to face the pain. Instead of pulling back, we push into the pain and then through it."[21]

The first stage of my healing was extremely grueling. I say *first stage* because I view healing as a lifelong process. Certainly the nine months I spent in the healing program, and the year afterward, proved the most intense. But healing is simply part of the journey toward spiritual maturity that God calls every believer to pursue. Though some periods of growth are more rapid and concentrated than others, a believer should always be in the process of transformation. First John 3:2–3 says that "what we will be has not yet been made known. But we know that when Christ appears, we shall be like him, for we shall see him as he is. All who have this hope in him purify themselves, just as he is pure" (NIV). Similarly, the apostle Paul asserted in Philippians 1:6, "And I am sure of this, that he who began a good work in you will bring it to completion at the day of Jesus Christ." Christians should always be growing in Christlikeness, and when we hit major roadblocks that impede our growth and threaten to derail us, God expects us to use the resources He's given us to overcome. But doing this is not easy.

For me, pushing through the intense emotional pain to a place of relative equilibrium took about eighteen months. But for those with more severe wounding, getting to that point is an almost unbearable ordeal that can take years. Admitting hurts, facing painful memories, confessing the sins we've committed and those committed against us, owning anger, and grieving losses can be excruciating and can even plunge some into depression. By God's grace, this depression is usually temporary, but it underscores just how difficult healing can be.

In a podcast discussion on this topic, Juli Slattery told me that it's common for life to get worse for those in need of healing before it gets better. "You can go through anywhere from six months to a couple of years just feeling like you're falling apart," she said. Understandably, she said people are often reluctant to enter this process. She likened the journey to healing to having a bad stomachache: "Part of you doesn't want to throw up because that's not a fun process. But the longer you keep that bacteria in your stomach, the more it's going to bug you and bug you and bug you. The process of getting it out isn't fun, but when you're done, you're free."[22]

That promise of freedom fueled me as I walked the road to healing. There was no way I could have endured that process without believing there was light at the end of the tunnel. That is the great solace of the Christian faith. Our suffering, when submitted to God, is always redemptive. He works all things together for our good.[23]

Jesus taught that if a seed falls to the ground and dies, it produces much fruit.[24] The apostle Paul wrote in Romans 5:3–4 that we should "glory in our sufferings, because we know that suffering produces perseverance; perseverance, character; and character, hope" (NIV). Suffering, for the Christian, always has meaning and purpose; it always produces something of value.

Chuck Colson wrote, "The real question is not whether we will suffer, but how we will react to suffering when it comes." Certainly, this is the case for those of us in need of healing. We can suffer in our dysfunction, addiction, or shame-induced paralysis. We can routinely choose escapes that offer momentarily relief but in the end only increase our pain and destroy our lives and the lives of those closest to us. Or, as Colson advises, "we can offer [our suffering] to God for His redemptive purposes." Colson understood suffering and redemption. He served seven months in a federal prison for his role in the Nixon administration's Watergate cover-up. God used that experience redemptively to spur Colson to start Prison Fellowship, the largest outreach to prisoners and their families in the United States. "This is the great truth Christians know," Colson wrote. "God will always use what we suffer for Christ's work of redemption if we let Him."[25]

Our example on this journey toward wholeness is Jesus. In Hebrews 12:2, we're told that Jesus "endured the cross" and all its shame "for the joy that was set before him." The entire time Jesus was being whipped, mocked, beaten, and torturously hung on a tree, He was thinking of the joy His suffering would achieve. He was thinking of the joy of our redemption—and of welcoming us back into fellowship with Himself, the Father, and the Holy Spirit. Just as this joy gave Jesus impetus to submit to suffering, we, too, should submit to suffering, trusting God to use it redemptively.

"The extended arms of Jesus on the cross illustrate the crucial first step in the healing process: Jesus opens himself to the excruciating pain," Seamands wrote. "He makes himself vulnerable. He holds nothing back. With his exposed heart and pain-racked body, Jesus embraces the agony of the cross. His outspread arms teach us that healing happens not by avoiding suffering but by accepting and actively bearing it."[26] This is a radical idea for Americans. So much of our lives revolve around avoiding pain. But Jesus said, "Whoever wants to be my disciple must deny themselves and take up their cross and follow me."[27]

As I walked the path toward healing, Jesus, this "man of sorrows" who was "acquainted with grief,"[28] was my model—and pressing into the pain was my cross. Throughout His life, Jesus was tempted to take shortcuts. When He was in the desert and racked with hunger from fasting forty days and nights, Satan appealed to Him to turn stones into bread. When that didn't work, Satan urged Jesus to throw Himself down from the temple.[29] But perhaps Jesus' greatest time of testing came in the Garden of Gethsemane. Knowing the agony that lay ahead, He still chose to embrace it. He said, "Not as I will, but as you will."[30]

Unfortunately there is no shortcut to healing. It involves brutal honesty—admitting the pain others have caused us, intentional or otherwise. It requires facing memories, even those memories we've been avoiding our whole lives. It means grieving losses and deprivations, forgiving those who have hurt us, and at times forgiving ourselves. It is a difficult road, but not an especially complicated one. It is simply following in the footsteps of our Master and trusting Him to deliver us safely to a better destination.

MY PATH TO HEALING

Many liken healing to peeling an onion: The Holy Spirit gives insight. You deal with it and experience freedom and joy. Then you discover there's more—another issue, or layer, that requires attention. After dealing with that issue, you discover there's another, and then another. And you continue with that process, revealing layer after layer, each time going deeper in your relationship with God and further in your personal transformation. Healing was definitely like that for me.

In the first few months, I was extremely eager to get to the root of my dysfunctional relationship with Sarah. Very quickly, I understood that it was tied to my relationship with my mother. It helped that my brother's confession about his boarding school experience had happened shortly before my experience with Sarah. With the Holy Spirit's help, I was quickly able to put two and two together and understand how my past and Sarah's particular dysfunction had combined into a perfect storm. But as I began to explore my childhood and the way it had shaped me, I discovered more.

During one of our small groups, I remembered a time when I was five years old and had gone to a friend's house for a sleepover. I was excited to go, but the minute the front door closed and my mother left, I panicked. I remembered frantically peering out the gold plastic sidelight on the side of the front door for a glimpse of my mother. I couldn't see anything, and I was terrified. To my knowledge, I didn't say anything to my friend or her parents. Perhaps by that time I had already learned to hide my feelings and to soothe myself. But the intensity of the emotion I felt as I recalled this memory caused me to suspect the memory was significant. Why had I been so panicked at my mother's leaving? What did that mean?

Several weeks later I relayed the incident to my mother, who was sick but still alive at the time. She then told me that when I was just eighteen months old, she and my dad had left me with a missionary couple while the rest of my family went on vacation for two weeks. Apparently my parents figured their vacation would be more enjoyable without a toddler in tow. The couple with whom they left me were loving Christians who adored children, so they assumed I would thoroughly enjoy my time in their care.

When she returned after two weeks, my mother said I wouldn't come to her. I had bonded to my temporary mom and cried when my biological mother tried to take me from her. I was stunned. I had recently learned about the importance of attachment and bonding in children and recognized that my failure to go to my mother marked a significant disruption. Experts in child development now recognize that a young child's need for her mother is as strong as the need for food, so separating from her for extended periods of time can be traumatic. It's especially difficult for children under the age of thirty-six months because they only understand two times—now and never. So when a mother is gone, they don't realize that she is returning.[31] When my mother didn't return for days, it's likely I concluded that she was gone forever and in desperation bonded with my mother substitute. This likely was very distressing for me and would explain why I panicked at my mother's departure several years later. It also further explained why I, as an adult, had developed a codependent tendency.

The next Wednesday, I relayed what I had learned to my small group. As we began to pray about it, the intensity of emotion returned. I felt the separation anxiety and utter loneliness I had sometimes experienced as a child. I sobbed and sobbed. But as they prayed, I felt this warmth and love reach deep into my soul. I could sense that God knew the depth of my pain. He didn't minimize it. He didn't tell me to suck it up. He simply wrapped His arms around me and let me know that He cared, and that despite the billions of people walking the planet, He saw and loved me.

Over the course of the next eighteen months, I had numerous experiences like that. God provided insight—sometimes revealing a memory that brought understanding, or a diseased attitude that required confession and repentance—and His presence produced healing. I once had a friend tell me that after months of counseling, he felt just as bad, or worse, than when he had started. Sure, the counseling had helped him understand why he was messed up, but understanding, in and of itself, doesn't solve anything. He likened the experience to pulling a tree up by its roots and inspecting them. Looking at the roots provided knowledge about the tree, but it didn't necessarily improve the health of that tree. I am so grateful that God placed me in a ministry that believed and ministered in the power of the Holy Spirit. Humanly speaking, these deep wounds are incurable. But with God, all things are possible.

CHOOSING TO BE FREE

God doesn't leave us interned in prisons of our own guilt, shame, and negative behavior patterns if we are willing to trust Him and walk with

Him through the healing process. If we do that, there are great rewards. Dr. Seamands reminds us that, in Christ, "the suffering we feared would be destructive becomes redemptive. Self-destroying, spirit-depleting suffering turns into self-enlarging, spirit-strengthening suffering."[32]

However, if we refuse to trust God and run from our healing, there are serious consequences. "If we are in a place where we're not willing to address the painful things in our life, then by and large, we're dictated by those painful things," Slattery said. "Those will dictate all your relationships. It will influence all of your decisions. It will influence your relationship with the Lord. . . . So, you're really living a compromised life if you allow the pain from the past to dictate your decisions today."[33]

I remember standing at the crossroads and having to choose between the road to healing and the road of escape. The road of escape looked easy, but I suspected it was a dead end. The road to healing looked difficult, but I trusted it led to a better destination. Jesus said, "Enter through the narrow gate. For wide is the gate and broad is the road that leads to destruction, and many enter through it. But small is the gate and narrow the road that leads to life, and only a few find it."[34] Everything that means anything to me today I would have lost had I chosen the escape route. I would have lost my family. I would have compromised my relationship with God. I would have forfeited my ministry. But I chose the narrow gate—or, to borrow from poet Robert Frost, "the one less traveled by, / And that has made all the difference."[35]

I emerged from that tumultuous yet fruitful season of intense healing as a changed person. Friends close to me said I became more compassionate than I had been before. I think that was their nice way of saying I was rather prideful and impatient before. After my healing experience, I was keenly aware of my frailty and of my need for God, and I was able to empathize with others on a whole new level. I also was gloriously free from the emotional dependency that had gripped me. I thank God that I have never experienced anything like that since, nor do I suspect I ever will again. But the journey is not over. God is still remaking me, and I am extremely grateful for His continued presence and intervention.

NINE

MARGINALIZING MOTHERHOOD

She was the attractive wife of a trailblazing megachurch pastor. She also had two beautiful children and a nice home in an affluent suburb. But Lynne Hybels, wife of Bill Hybels, senior pastor of Willow Creek Community Church, was miserable. That's according to the couple's daughter Shauna Niequist, who told her mother's story at a conference I attended in 2014.

"My dad was at church a lot; my mom was at home always," Niequist recounted. "She was an excellent caregiver, an attentive and gentle mother, a loving parent. But, in her own words, she was not happy. We had a good, good mom, but we did not have a happy one. Seventeen years after becoming a pastor's wife, she walked into a counselor's office and said, 'I don't have any idea who I am anymore. Something serious has to change.'"[1]

For Hybels, change meant finding her voice and pursuing a meaningful vocation outside the home. She had lost herself in the day-to-day demands of being a mother, and it wasn't until she began exploring her gifts and passions—serving in the inner city and taking trips to Latin America—that she awakened to who she really was.

"Little by little, my mom began to look inside to consider for the first time in almost twenty years what it was she really loved—what she was made to do," Niequist said.

> Through trial and error, through counseling, through prayer and friendship and hard work, she rediscovered the gifts and the passions that drew her to social work and to church-planting, so many years ago. . . . And, what she found is that she felt more alive in a squalid shanty town in Mexico, passing out canned peaches to barefoot, beautiful children, than she did in the affluent suburbs that we lived in. She found that her gifts, the way God made her, were about helping people in need, not administrating carpool schedules.[2]

Shauna was fourteen when her mother underwent this transformation from stay-at-home mom to international activist, and it profoundly affected her. "I watched my mother come alive," she said. "The life I was seeing in her for the first time was so inspiring, I wanted to follow that journey." Apparently Lynne and Bill Hybels now want others to follow that journey too. Shauna said her parents deeply regret that they allowed "the logistical challenge of raising young children" to fall primarily on Lynne and to stifle her pursuits. She added that they now urge young couples not to repeat their mistakes, but instead to "work hard to find creative solutions for the practical concerns of child-raising, so that both parents can pursue their callings."

Shauna explained that she and her husband, Aaron Niequist, are prime examples of this new model. The couple has two young children, while maintaining two high-profile careers. Aaron is on staff at Willow Creek as a worship leader, writes and records original music, and speaks at churches. Shauna is the author of multiple books and tours the country, speaking at women's events. Shauna admitted that making "space for two callings in one home and one marriage" can be challenging.

> But if I tried to put my calling on hold for any amount of time, my mother would be the first one to show up on my doorstep and say, "No way! I didn't walk that long path of depression and passionless days so that you can recreate them." . . . She would say, "Write till your fingers bleed, tell stories till your voice runs out because it's what you were made to do—mother or not, woman or not." If I tried to shelve my gifts for any amount of time, if I tried to give back the voice and the calling God gave me, she would be the first in line to say, "Get back to work because it fills you, because you love it, because it helps people, because you're you when you do it!"[3]

REGRETS

Shauna's message was well received at the conference I attended, and a video of her talk, posted on YouTube, has received more than thirty thousand views. I was disturbed by it though. Granted, I probably heard Shauna's message with different ears than many of the people at the conference. Most of them were young evangelical leaders—a good ten to fifteen years younger than me—so it's likely that most of them still had young children at home. I, on the other hand, had two sons attending colleges in different states, and only my daughter remained at home with my husband and me. Like Lynne I had regrets, but they were very different.

I didn't regret that I had failed to chase my dreams or develop my gifts. I had pursued my passions though, in my late twenties, I left a potentially high-powered career in TV news to pursue motherhood and ministry. That transition had been hard. At the same time I left my job, our family also moved to a different town. I had expected to make friends with lots of moms in our new community, but that didn't happen—at least, not immediately. Instead, I remember going to playgrounds with my two-year-old son and finding them deserted. It was as if we were living in a mommy-toddler ghost town. Our previous home (a rented two-flat) had been on Chicago's pricey North Shore. The playgrounds there were full, but almost exclusively populated by nannies with other people's children. I thought it would be different moving to a predominantly middle-class neighborhood. And it was, just not in the way I had expected. I soon discovered that most of the kids in our new community were in day care all day, so my stay-at-home life was at first solitary.

Desperate to connect with other moms and find playmates for my son, I enrolled in a couple of park district classes. There I found other moms, but we often had very little in common. I had just left a job in a bustling Chicago newsroom, where my colleagues and I would routinely discuss world events and local politics. Now I was surrounded by moms who wanted to discuss favorite recipes, decorating ideas, and their kids' sleep schedules. There's nothing wrong with discussing those things, but at the time I felt like a fish out of water. I panicked. Was this what my life now would be like? Just a few months prior, I had been hobnobbing with high-ranking politicians and local media personalities. Now I was sitting in a circle, singing "Itsy Bitsy Spider," and it was frightening.

If it hadn't been for youth ministry, I'm not sure I would have survived my first few years as a stay-at-home mom. For six of my thirteen years at home, youth ministry was an outlet for my creative energies and a way to connect with the mission of the local church. Plus, it worked well with my family's schedule. I would often plan events and write talks during my kids' nap times. Many of our meetings with the youth and youth leaders occurred at night after our kids went to bed. Other events, such as trips and retreats, would require us to leave home for several days, but rather than hire a babysitter, we would take our kids with us. That enriched the lives of everyone involved. Our kids loved hanging out with the teenagers, and the teenagers enjoyed being with our kids and watching how a Christian family lived and interacted.

Given my experience, I can understand how someone like Lynne Hybels might find stay-at-home mothering restrictive and even soul crushing. The role can be lonely, and at times mind-numbing—especially when children are young. But encouraging women to find fulfillment outside the home doesn't necessarily solve this problem. In fact, it can exacerbate it. The message that moms must work to be complete can make those who stay at home feel inadequate. Even worse, it can compel women to take on too much, often at the expense of their children.

For me, motherhood was a role that eventually became comfortable. One of the by-products of the healing process I went through was a new level of peace with being a mom. I felt more secure than ever in my identity in Christ, and I didn't need a job or position to bolster it. After six years of working in youth ministry, I resigned and began doing something I had never considered before—homeschooling my kids. That period lasted four years, and I don't regret a single sacrifice I made to homeschool my kids. What I do regret is conceding when our boys wanted to return to public school so they could play sports. My husband and I thought we could guide their education and counter the errant ideas they encountered at school, but the immersion in a thoroughly anti-Christian worldview confused them and wreaked havoc on their spiritual lives. Our daughter, on the other hand, went to a small Christian school and thrived.

When my kids returned to school, I returned to work, this time in Christian radio. Initially, working seemed quite manageable. But when problems began to surface with our boys, I didn't have the reserves these issues required. My job required me to commute into the city, and though I was able to leave early in the morning and return by the time my kids came home, I was exhausted most evenings. Yes, I was able to put a meal on the table, but I was less patient and more irritable—and so was my husband. My working and commuting put extra strain on him. Now, he was the one who had to get the kids up in the morning and out the door, which was no small feat. And he had to handle more evening commitments because my early start time meant getting to bed by 9:00 p.m.

So, at one of the most critical junctures in our boys' spiritual development, my husband and I were the most distracted. We missed warning signs we normally would have noticed, and we sometimes reacted poorly to crises due to the high levels of stress. If I had to do it over again, I would have delayed my return to work and continued to homeschool, or sent our boys to a nearby Christian school despite its scant sports program. God has redeemed many of the effects of those chaotic years. My boys are now fine young men I am proud to call sons, and my daughter is developing into a beautiful, godly woman. I now recognize the errors in my mothering, and I would love to go back and correct them. But I can't. No one can.

Shauna asserted that "everyone wins when women discover and live out of the gifts and the passions that God gave them." There's certainly truth in that statement. Growing up, I remember watching my mother blossom and bless many people in my church, serving as the superintendent of Sunday school—a job that capitalized on her strong Bible teaching and administrative skills. But I have also seen how pursuing my passions can hurt my family, or how other women have decimated their families by putting their outside "callings" first. Certainly fathers can do this too. But as the primary nurturers and managers of the home, mothers have a unique responsibility to be readily available to their children. When mothers are regularly absent, their children suffer profoundly.

During my youth ministry years, I remember receiving several gut-wrenching calls from a woman pastor who pleaded with me to help save her teenage daughters. Through tears she confessed to me that she had neglected her family and lost her girls. She had thought she had been serving the Lord. She had thought she had been fulfilling her dream. But when her kids deserted God and her family, she realized she had lost what was most precious—her own children.

That redefines regret. It is one thing to look back regretfully on some unfulfilling years spent buried in kids' activities and helping with homework. It's another to wake up one morning and realize that you failed at the most important task God gave you—and you have two lost daughters as a result.

After Shauna's talk I happened to bump into a young stay-at-home mother while waiting in a long bathroom line. I asked her what she thought of the talk, and she hemmed and hawed, seeming unsure of how much she should disclose to a total stranger. Then she asked me what I thought, and I told her, "I'm pushing fifty right now. I have two grown sons and a daughter in middle school. I also have a career in radio, speaking, and writing. I love my vocation. But it pales in comparison to my family. You get one shot at raising your children. Careers can wait; your kids' childhoods cannot." We then reached the front of the line and parted ways. But as I was leaving the conference hall about three hours later, I saw the young mother I had met in the bathroom line waiting by one of the exits. As I approached, she said to me with tears in her eyes, "Oh, I was hoping I'd find you! I just wanted to say thank you for what you said. I really needed to hear that."

IS MOTHERHOOD ENOUGH?

Many moms today need to hear that motherhood is worth sacrific-ing some of their best years. Unfortunately, that's not what they're hearing—not from society, and not from the church. Instead they're hearing that full-time motherhood is a waste of their lives and a capit-ulation to tradition and patriarchy. It's fine for women to get married and have babies, but not at the expense of their careers and passions. So when Michelle Obama, for example, announced in 2008 that she intended to be "mom-in-chief," feminists like lawyer and author Linda Hirshman decried the First Lady for "letting down the team."[4] Similarly, feminist and Yale research fellow Emily Bazelon lamented, "Why does mom-in-chief have to be the most important thing this strong, vibrant woman tells us about herself as she flexes the strange but considerable power of the office of first lady?"[5]

These kinds of messages have been bombarding women since the sixties, when feminists such as Betty Friedan burst onto the scene comparing women who dream of being housewives to "the mil-lions who walked to their own death in the concentration camps."[6] Traditionally, the church has resisted this message and held mother-hood in high regard, perhaps even too high of a regard. Some have rightly noted that referring to motherhood as a woman's highest call-ing, as some churches do, has communicated to single women that their lives are less important. Now the pendulum seems to have swung in the other direction. Christian stay-at-home mothers are being told that their callings are somehow incomplete if not supplemented with outside pursuits. So, both inside the church and outside, these moth-ers are bombarded with messages that make them feel as if their work is inadequate and unimportant.

In an interview about her book *A Woman's Place*, Katelyn Beaty, a Christian feminist who's thirtysomething and single, asserted that all women have a responsibility to work outside the home—kids or no kids. "All women are called to have influence—cultural influence outside of the private sphere of the home," Beaty said. "It wouldn't necessarily have to be a career track, but certainly all Christians, including all Christian women, are called to have cultural influence outside the home."

Beaty said she used to believe that a mother's "central call" was to stay at home with children. But her views have changed. If she were to get married and have children today, she would look for a way to continue working. She urged Christian mothers to assess their talents and find ways to use them outside the home. To do anything less would essentially mean abdicating their God-given responsibility to impact culture.[7]

In her book, Beaty supported her promotion of work outside the home by citing what's known as the cultural mandate. This is the belief, based on Genesis 1–3, that God ordained all bearers of His image, men and women alike, to be creators of culture. God commanded Adam and Eve to "be fruitful and increase in number; fill the earth and subdue it."[8] When men and women use their natural abilities to harness nature and to build societies, we fulfill this command. Conversely, when we bury our talents, we violate this command, which Beaty asserted can actually cause us emotional and spiritual harm. "If we take Genesis 1–3 at face value," she wrote, we "know that when women can't or don't 'work with willing hands' . . . their Imago Dei is dimmed, and so is their own well-being" since to live fully into our image bearing is necessarily to live with wholeness, purpose, and delight.[9]

Beaty further argued that stay-at-home motherhood is not a role prescribed in Scripture, but rather a reductionist role created by the

Industrial Revolution. Before the Industrial Revolution, economic activity was centered in the home. Although differences certainly existed between the functions of men and women, they worked hand in hand not only to provide for their families, but also to raise their children. The Industrial Revolution moved work outside the home and created a strict division of labor. Men primarily engaged in the creative work outside the home, and women were relegated to raising kids and managing the affairs of the home.[10]

This reduced role, Beaty asserted, has led to a legion of problems. More specifically, it has led to what Betty Friedan termed "the problem that has no name." This is a sense among middle-class housewives that they are "wasting away" because their "intellect, skills and passions" are not finding expression in the larger culture.[11]

Certainly Beaty has a point about the Industrial Revolution negatively impacting families and motherhood. By moving work outside the home, it divided the family unit and reduced the mother's ability to contribute to economic activity. I wish our society was different and that our work as mothers could be more easily integrated with professional work. But it's not, and women working outside the home won't change that. It's simply going to mean that mothers trade some of the time and influence they would have invested in their families and invest those precious commodities elsewhere.

Is the malaise both Beaty and Friedan witnessed in women truly the result of stay-at-home mothers lacking the opportunity to fulfill the cultural mandate? The first part of the cultural mandate as mentioned in Genesis has nothing to do with pursuing work outside the home, but is focused entirely on procreation. God said, "Be fruitful and increase in number; fill the earth." What Beaty's analysis overlooks is that even in its most reduced form, motherhood is one of the most crucial roles in all of culture. The family is the fundamental building block of society, so nurturing the next generation is essential if societies are to thrive. Stay-at-home mothers are fulfilling the cultural mandate whether they work outside the home or not.

Beaty admitted this point in her article on *The Feminine Mystique*. Referencing a book written by *Christianity Today* executive editor Andy Crouch, she wrote, "A family is a little civilization unto itself, with its own history, customs, and language, and mothers have a crucial role in shaping the generations who lead the nations."[12] It's odd that Beaty would simultaneously make such strong statements indicating that devoting oneself solely to motherhood is somehow insufficient.

Still, how do we account for mothers' seeming unhappiness? I had an opportunity to talk with Beaty, and she asked me what I would suggest for these unhappy mothers. Would I encourage them to pursue outside interests? Before I prescribe a remedy, I suggested that we first must diagnose the true cause of unhappiness. There are endless possible causes of mothers' emotional distress, ranging from unhappy marriages to unhealed emotional wounds to lack of personal care. But I don't believe mothers' unhappiness has anything to do with not fulfilling the cultural mandate. However, it may have everything to do with our culture.

I have a friend whose mother felt acutely unhappy with motherhood in the seventies. After years of meeting in women's groups and trying to find her unique voice and identity, she took the advice of feminists to pursue interests outside her home and divorced her husband. Then, when my friend and his older brother were just eleven and thirteen, she moved two thousand miles away to try and find herself. She spent decades exploring different self-help programs and New Age religion. She studied and got two master's degrees. Eventually she remarried and converted to Catholicism, but she divorced again. Today she is single, distant from both her sons, and filled with regret.

Obviously this woman's problem wasn't rooted in her failure to pursue outside interests, because doing so didn't solve her problem; it actually destroyed her life and damaged her children. Her unhappiness was not rooted in her circumstance—that is, motherhood and domesticity—but in the way she viewed her circumstance.

Today there's an entire movement among mothers who seemingly are experiencing "the problem with no name" on steroids. Except now it has a name. It's called *baby regret*. Laura, a thirty-seven-year-old journalist based in Los Angeles, told a reporter for *Marie Claire* that she wishes she'd never had a child.

> The regret hit me when the grandmas went home and my husband went back to the office and I was on my own with him. I realized that this was my life now—and it was unbearable. . . . I hated, hated, hated the situation I found myself in. I think the word for what I felt is "trapped." After I had a kid, I realized I hated being the mother to an infant, but by then it was too late. I couldn't walk away and still live with myself, but I also couldn't stand it. I felt like my life was basically a middle-class prison.

Similarly, Ananya, a thirty-eight-year-old freelance writer and editor, said she regrets motherhood because of all the missed opportunities it's caused: "I wonder if my accomplishments would be more spectacular. Would I have written my second or third book? . . . I feel motherhood has slowed me down so much."[13]

As Christians, we're aghast at these sentiments and selfish decisions. Rejecting motherhood to pursue personal freedom and careerism is not at all what Beaty or Hybels or Niequist are promoting. But the diagnosis of women's unhappiness and the suggested remedy are eerily similar. All diagnose the problem as women not using their intellects and skills in the larger culture. The solution therefore is to find places outside the home where they can do so. The only difference between the two models, secular and Christian, is one of degrees. Unlike the young Lynne Hybels, the women experiencing baby regret already have outside vocations. These outside pursuits simply aren't enough to satiate their cravings for personal freedom and significance.

Reflecting on this phenomenon, Catholic writer Jennifer Hartline noted, "This is evidence of a culture that has shrunk into a real smallness of being. So small that there is only room for one: I. It is an atrophy of the deepest heart. It is a caving in of ourselves, into a cage of mirrors where all we can see is our sad reflection."[14] The bottom line is that we live in a culture that defines significance in an individualistic way. We can see the connection between significance and service only if it fits into a larger picture of our personal visions and callings. If our service simply builds into the soul of another, even if we love that other person, we somehow lose the connection. And if our service involves menial acts of love and mercy, rather than grandiose ones, we fail to see how our "work with willing hands" fulfills the cultural mandate. We need to recapture a biblical understanding of motherhood as a noble and divine calling where women flourish and discover their purposes, rather than pursue their passions.

A NOBLE AND DIVINE CALLING

Practically every month for more than thirty years, I, like most other women on this earth, go through a weeklong cycle that reminds me that I was made to bear children. When I someday grow too old for this monthly reminder, I will still have the reminders stamped on my body. I like to think of them as red badges of courage—signs that I carried three beautiful souls to full term. I am not interested in having them removed with lasers or some medical or surgical intervention. They are my glory, and I embrace them fully.

My husband has no similar reminders. Though he has been a wonderful and attentive father, his participation in our children's conception and prenatal development was rather brief. For our children's first few months, I provided something for them through nursing that he couldn't possibly provide. Today, society likes to pretend that women and men play essentially the same role in the care and nurture of children, but my body tells me otherwise. As John Paul II noted, "The whole constitution of woman's body is made for motherhood."[15] And, since John Paul believed the body reveals the person, he taught that women's biology speaks volumes about the dignity and nature of women. Bearing and nurturing children is one of our unique blessings and honors. Adam named his wife Eve, which means "life-giver," and that role is essential to who women are. At the sight of Jesus a woman called out, "Blessed is the mother who gave you birth and nursed you."[16] Motherhood is at the core of our identity as women. And, whether we bear biological children or not, nurturing is fundamental to who we are.

We see this truth woven throughout the pages of Scripture. In the Old Testament, women are often highlighted because of the children they bear. Sarah, for example, becomes the mother of a nation by bearing Isaac when she's in her nineties. Hannah provides Israel with a godly prophet after pleading with God to open her womb.

In the New Testament, the apostle Paul urges women to be faithful mothers as a sign of godliness. In 1 Timothy 5:14, Paul counsels "younger widows to marry, to have children, to manage their homes" (NIV). For a widow to qualify for financial support, he requires that she have a history of being "faithful to her husband," and "known for her good deeds, such as bringing up children."[17] This theme continues in Titus 2:4–5. There Paul tells the older women to "urge the younger women to love their husbands and children, to be self-controlled and pure, to be busy at home" (NIV). In all these passages, Paul offers no similar encouragement for men, but seems to be making a gender-specific charge.

God values motherhood because He values children and is critically concerned with transferring the faith from one generation to another. Malachi 2:15 says, "And what was the one God seeking? Godly offspring." In Deuteronomy 11–12, God instructs parents to teach the law to the next generation, "so that it may always go well with you and your children after you" (12:28 NIV). Mothers play a critical role in teaching faith to children. Timothy, one of Paul's key partners in ministry, is a prime example of what the influence of a godly mother, and even grandmother, can do. "I am reminded of your sincere faith," Paul wrote to Timothy, "which first lived in your grandmother Lois and in your mother Eunice and, I am persuaded, now lives in you also."[18]

The thought that motherhood is somehow unworthy of a woman's complete energy is absent in Scripture, and it should be absent in the church. As Pastor John MacArthur once said, "To be a mother is by no means second class. Men may have the authority in the home, but the women have the influence. The mother, more than the father, is the one who molds and shapes those little lives from day one."[19]

About 150 years ago, William Ross Wallace acknowledged the immense influence of mothers in his famous poem "The Hand That Rocks the Cradle." The poem noted that mothers shape the hearts and minds of their children, and by extension, "rule the world." They, more than anyone else, can influence the next generation "for the good or evil," and "keep the young heart open always to the breath of God."[20] This is why President Theodore Roosevelt said, "The good mother, the wise mother . . . is more important to the community than even the ablest man; her career is more worthy of honor and is more useful to the community than the career of any man, no matter how successful."[21]

Perhaps the most famous mother in Scripture, other than Mary, is the Proverbs 31 Woman. This woman is often upheld as a model for working mothers, and in some ways she is. She provides food and clothes for her family, but she also sells the clothes she's made and turns a profit by trading items in the marketplace. Yet she does not work outside her home to find meaning or fulfillment; she leverages her many skills for the good of her family.

As Candice Watters, author and cocreator of Focus on the Family's *Boundless* webzine, explains, the Proverbs 31 Woman demonstrates that Christian womanhood can include "more than caring for home and hearth, but never less. . . . Proverbs 31 is not the model for a 1950s America that guided women away from the family farm or trade and into domestic cul-de-sacs. Nor is it a contemporary model that encourages women to give their primary time and best attention to the workplace. Rather, it is a vision of a thriving and fruitful life with home as the hub."[22]

This is the true vision of biblical motherhood and the biblical home. The home is not a prison that mothers need to escape occasionally or they'll wither and their gifts will go to waste. It is presented as a flourishing and fruitful garden that mothers tend and nurture—and in which they find great purpose and delight. This service may involve menial tasks, such as cooking or sewing, but it demands a woman's full creative potential. Whether menial or complex, all of a mother's tasks have meaning because they serve a great and noble purpose. Unfortunately many Christian women seem to have forgotten this noble purpose.

PURPOSE OVER PASSIONS

Today Christian leaders are constantly urging women to follow their passions. Writer, speaker, and therapist Julia Mateer wrote in *Gifted for Leadership*, "Knowing your passion is the key to discovering your calling." She then offered the following questions to help women "uncover their passion" so they can discover their mission and calling:

1. If money were not an issue, what would you do with your time?
2. What do you love to do? What do you hate to do?
3. What gives you energy? What drains the life out of you?
4. What do you want to change, shape, and leave better than you found it?
5. What segment of the population are you drawn to help?
6. What do you want to experience, witness, and learn?[23]

I can just imagine how I would have answered those questions when my kids were toddlers. Most of my answers would likely have involved escaping to quiet and serene locations, time alone with my husband, and investing in ministry where I was experiencing a lot of immediate success. None of them would have led me to embracing motherhood because every single one of Mateer's questions focused on self. What do *you* want . . . ? What do *you* love . . . ? Granted, we mothers intensely love our children, but motherhood requires dying to self. It requires sacrificing what we want and what we find fulfilling for what someone else needs. Jesus said, "Whoever loses his life for my sake will find it,"[24] so fulfillment, according to Jesus, is not found in discovering and pursuing passions but in sacrificing ourselves for a higher purpose. Christians should be purpose driven, not passion driven.

Caroline Beaton, a twentysomething freelance author who admitted she's "hunting meaning . . . but unsatisfied," noted in an article for *Forbes* that "following your passion is a deceptively slow, uncertain way to purpose."[25] Passion is self-oriented and pleasure oriented, and tends to be short-term. Quoting a study published in *Self and Identity*,[26] she wrote that passion is "a strong inclination toward a self-defining activity that one loves, values, and in which one invests a substantial amount of time and energy." Or, as branding strategist Terri Trespicio explained in a TEDx talk, "Passion is not a plan. Passion is a feeling, and feelings change."[27]

Purpose, on the other hand, is others oriented. According to one Stanford study, people with "meaning mindsets 'seek connections, give to others, and orient themselves to a larger purpose.'"[28] Purpose tends to be long-term, Beaton noted, and also gives "more weight to meaning than pleasure." Purpose may be connected to passion, but after years spent chasing her passions, Beaton concluded, "Don't expect [passion] to produce your purpose."[29]

All the talk among Christian women today about following their passions sounds an awful lot like seeking Abraham Maslow's self-actualization, the desire to attain our full potential once all our basic needs are met. Are we really seeking God's calling? Or are we desperately seeking importance and fulfillment? Could it be that we are so desperately seeking to find and fulfill our passions because we have lost sight of our purpose?

Once a woman becomes a mother, she has no greater kingdom purpose than molding the life of her child. That child, for whom Christ gave His life, is dependent on her for his or her well-being. And there is no one else on the face of the earth who can play the role that a mother plays in the life of her child. No one. As one of my pastors once said to me when I was wrestling with whether or not to work,

"Julie, God can find someone else to do your job, but you're the only one who can be a mother to your child."

Motherhood is an incredibly high calling, and when mothers serve their families, they serve the kingdom of God. When they sideline their passions for a season, they are not wasting their lives; they are trusting Jesus' words that "whoever loses their life for me will find it."[30]

In my twenty-five years of motherhood, I have found that passion generally follows purpose, not vice versa. The more I understand and embrace God's call on my life to love and nurture my children, the more passionate about motherhood I become. Making dinner, which I once considered a chore, becomes an act of supreme importance. It is a way God has ordained for me to strengthen our family bonds and to transmit kingdom beliefs and values to the next generation. Giving the gift of my presence while we eat that dinner nourishes the souls of my children and husband. It communicates to them that they are significant and worthy of my complete attention. Sure, I can impact others to some extent when I host a radio show. But nowhere will my impact be more profound than with my own children.

As G. K. Chesterton wrote in *What's Wrong with the World*:

When people begin to talk about [motherhood] as not merely difficult but trivial and dreary, I simply give up the question. For I cannot with the utmost energy of imagination conceive what they mean. . . . How can it be a large career to tell other people's children about the Rule of Three, and a small career to tell one's own children about the universe? How can it be broad to be the same thing to everyone, and narrow to be everything to someone? No; a woman's function is laborious, but because it is gigantic, not because it is minute. I will pity Mrs. Jones for the hugeness of her task; I will never pity her for its smallness.[31]

Motherhood is significant for yet another reason. Over the past twenty-five years, I have learned that not only does God use motherhood to change our children, but He also uses it to change us. I once read about a bumper sticker that said, "My children saved me from toxic self-absorption,"[32] and I laughed—and simultaneously thanked God. We live in a culture that constantly pushes us toward narcissism—and frankly, that's precisely what the emphasis on pursuing our passions does too. But motherhood, unlike anything else I know, has the power to pull us outside of ourselves. It's one of the only situations where we're capable of loving someone more than we love ourselves, and we practice a level of servanthood that we would otherwise find impossible. Motherhood allows us to grow at an exponential rate and to be molded into Christ's image. So much of who I am today, which enables me to do the ministry I do, was developed in the crucible of motherhood.

TODAY'S "PROBLEM WITH NO NAME"

As women increasingly have sought their own happiness, it has become more elusive. Despite all our advancements and achievements, we are not generally happier than our mothers or our grandmothers. We are simply more stressed, more driven, and more relationally disconnected.

Besides forgetting the spiritual principle that we find our lives by losing them, women have also forgotten another key reality—one that author Danielle Crittenden articulates in her book, *What Our Mothers Didn't Tell Us: Why Happiness Eludes the Modern Woman*:

If previous generations of women were raised to believe that they could only realize themselves within the roles of wife and mother, now the opposite is thought true: It's only *outside* these roles that we are able to realize our full potential and worth as human beings....

The modern problem with no name is, I believe, exactly the reverse of the old one: While we now recognize that women are human, we blind ourselves to the fact that we are also women. If we feel stunted and oppressed when denied the chance to realize our human potential, we suffer every bit as much when we cut off from those aspects of life that are distinctly and uniquely female.[33]

Today, women assume that what fulfills men also fulfills women. It doesn't. Yes, women enjoy work as men do, but it fulfills us to a lesser degree. What fulfills us most is close relational connection. A unique forty-year study called the Study of Mathematically Precocious Youth (SMPY) provides evidence of this. The study tracked more than sixteen hundred mathematically gifted boys and girls from their childhood in the seventies to their midlives in 2012. The study found that both the males and the females achieved similar levels of education, but when they began working, a significant gender gap developed.

The men in the study worked on average eleven hours more per week than the women, who generally adhered to a forty-hour workweek. Not surprisingly, the men in their middle-aged years made significantly more money than the women made during their same time of life. But what was especially revealing was why the men and the women made the different life choices they did. When asked what they valued most, the men said full-time work, making an impact, and earning a high income; the women said part-time work, community and family involvement, and time for close relationships.[34]

Men and women do not want the same things, at least not equally. Regardless of what culture says, women want close relationships more than they want careers. We want husbands and children and deep personal connections. Yet culture's devaluation of these things has cut us off from these desires until pretty late in life, when obtaining families is much more difficult. Today, it's not uncommon for a thirty-five-year-old single career woman to find herself suddenly possessed by a desire to have a family but lacking any serious suitors. Exacerbating the problem is the fact that today there are only eighty-five men for every one hundred women who are twenty-five to thirty-five years old and who are college educated.[35]

I got married young—at age twenty—but the urge to bear children came later. When it came, it was powerful. I had been married for six years and was happily pursuing my career goals. Then, out of the blue, I wanted a baby and could think of little else. After my first child was born, all I wanted to do for the first six months was be at home with him. When I finally returned to working part-time, I found that the entire time I was at work, my mind was fixed on my young son.

Rather than fighting these natural urges, maybe we women should start cooperating with them. Maybe we need to accept that God wired us to find our greatest fulfillment in nurturing others and pursue that. For most of us, this means embracing the role of wife and mother, but not for all. I have a single friend whom I met more than thirty-five years ago on a summer missions trip and have maintained contact with ever since. To me, she is Linda. But, to dozens of younger men and women, she is "Mama Lou." Though Mama Lou never married or bore children, she has mentored and cared for dozens of young people she's met through youth ministry and missions trips. She's even started a small outreach in Africa, diverting a significant percentage of her income as a nurse to support gospel work in a remote village there.

My single friend Jana, who's a professor at a Christian college, mentors dozens of women and men. Because of her single status, she has the time to pour into other people's lives in a way those of us raising biological children cannot. Jana and Mama Lou are every bit as much mothers as I am. They have done precisely what God instructs childless women to do in Isaiah 54:1–3:

> *"Sing, barren woman,*
> *you who never bore a child . . .*
> *because more are the children of the desolate woman*
> *than of her who has a husband," says the* Lord.
> *"Enlarge the place of your tent,*
> *stretch your tent curtains wide,*
> *do not hold back;*
> *lengthen your cords,*
> *strengthen your stakes.*
> *For you will spread out to the right and to the left;*
> *your descendants will dispossess nations*
> *and settle in their desolate cities.* (NIV)

Here, God is encouraging childless women to exert their maternal influence—to nurture the neglected and lost, to find those who need love and direction, and to gather them under their wings. In doing so they can have incredible impact; those they have mothered may even change the direction of nations![36]

God has given all women a special gift to love and nurture, and none of us—married or not, childless or not—should let this gift go to waste. This is the normative call for all women. Rather than feeling an obligation to work outside the home, we should feel an obligation to love and to nurture—and to bless society with this unique gift God has given us. As Darrow L. Miller wrote in *Nurturing the Nations*, "The death of motherhood leads very quickly to the death of nations."[37] We are literally experiencing this death of motherhood and of nations in many countries, particularly Western ones, as the birthrate is plummeting to below replacement rates.[38] We're experiencing the death of motherhood in a spiritual sense, as well.

"In the materially impoverished world there is little sense of nurturing a child for the future," Miller wrote. "And, a selfish generation in the rich world thinks largely of personal fulfillment: *How might I have a child with the greatest of convenience, putting the child in daycare and getting back to 'my career' as soon as possible?* These mindsets limit or demean the glory of female and motherhood and, in doing so, discount the motherly heart of God."[39]

As women, we must show the glory of the feminine to the world. God has manifested this aspect of Himself in us, and if we fail to honor it and cherish it, we impoverish our world. But if we embrace motherhood, our very existence speaks prophetically to an overly masculinized and utilitarian world. Production is not all-important; people are. Doing is not most essential to personhood; being and relationship are. Our society desperately needs mothers today, and if we abdicate this role or minimize it, the results will be devastating—not just to us, but to society.

CAN WE HAVE IT ALL?

As a kid growing up in the eighties, I heard a steady stream of messages that, as a woman, I could have it all—a great family and a great career. The iconic commercial by Enjoli perfume became women's anthem: "I can bring home the bacon, fry it up in a pan. And never let you forget you're a man—'cause I'm a woman by Enjoli!" Girl power was all about doing it all and having it all—and as a young person, I bought it hook, line, and sinker. That is, until I actually had young kids and a job and realized the strain it put on a home.

One of the hardest things for me to accept in life has been my limitations. I almost always bite off more than I can chew. It has been a struggle for me to say no to opportunities, especially career opportunities, but I have learned, sometimes the hard way, that I can't be a good mom and a relentlessly busy one. As Crittenden noted in her book, the maternal tension between work and home is "not due to a simple shortage of hours. Rather, it's an *existential* lack of time, a feeling of constantly being pulled . . . between two highly pressured worlds."[40] As moms, what are we going to sacrifice? For some moms, working isn't a choice; it's a necessity. They would gladly trade places with a stay-at-home mom if they didn't need the paycheck. However, one tragedy of our current era is that many moms are shortchanging their children and husbands for no apparent reason other than their need to feel significant. Before them lies a job of immeasurable significance, yet they are eschewing it for lesser callings.

About two years after her talk at Q, Shauna Niequist published a raw and vulnerable book in which she admitted that juggling her demanding career and family left her feeling worn-out, spiritually thin, and miserable. Reflecting on a rare evening she spent connecting with close girlfriends who, like her, were mothers with demanding careers, she wrote, "There we were, utterly resigned to lives that feel overly busy and pressurized, disconnected and exhausted." Then, very tellingly, she recounted a discussion she and her husband had with her son, Henry, during an equally rare evening they spent together playing Legos. The two asked Henry what he wanted for the upcoming year. They anticipated he might say more adventures, trips, or soccer leagues. But instead, he said simply, "More this . . . more time together like this. And at home. I like it when we're all together at home."[41]

That's precisely what our children want, and it's precisely what our families need. They want us fully present in the day-to-day, week-to-week, seemingly mundane, but gloriously significant life of our home. To Niequist's credit, she listened to her son and to her own spirit. Her entire book is about "leaving behind frantic for a simpler, more soulful way of living."

I am extremely grateful today that I was able to stay home with my kids for thirteen years. Not a single day goes by that I wish I had traded those years invested in my children with years invested in a career. Today, with two grown sons and a daughter in high school, I have a job, but it's an extremely flexible one. I do almost all my writing and preparation for my radio show at home while my daughter is in school. Other than Saturday mornings when I host my radio show and occasional outside speaking engagements, I am home when my family is home.

Still, I can't imagine doing what I'm doing today if my children were still young. I'd have to hire a babysitter to get anything done, which I suppose would be feasible. But then my children would be spending the better part of their waking hours with someone other than me. That person would become extremely influential in their lives, and I would become less influential, sacrificing thousands of hours that could be invested in relationship but instead would be devoted to work.

This isn't to say that women can't pursue interests outside our homes. We can, but shouldn't do so at the expense of our families or because we deem our vocations as mothers to be insufficiently satisfying. Candice Watters offers helpful advice for women seeking to strike a balance between jobs, volunteer work, and family: "What are the things only you, as a mom, can do?" she asks.

Do those things. And, if you have extra capacity, energy, and opportunity for outside pursuits, do those things, too . . . There's always more to do in a day than can be done. But ask yourself, of all the balls you juggle—mothering, working, time with friends, entertainment, church commitments, etc., which are the ones you never, or rarely drop? Which is the first to fall? If you find yourself cheating your kids in order to fulfill commitments at work, you're likely crossing that line. Of all the balls you might drop, kids, especially young children, suffer most from a fall.[42]

That is sobering advice all of us mothers need to heed. Much more than our personal fulfillment or passions are at stake. The fates of our families hang in the balance. The fates of our nations hang in the balance.

TEN

THE GLORIOUS BECOMING

An inch of snow blanketed the ground on the morning of April 2, 2002—a rare occurrence in April, even in Chicago. But this was no ordinary morning. This was the morning my daughter, Elia, entered the world. I'm sure many mothers who gave birth in Chicago on that day believed God sent the snow just for them and their beautiful babies. And who knows? Maybe He did. Maybe He sent it for all of us. But to me, the snow was a sign of God's goodness to my family and me, a reminder that He covers us with His purity and beauty and never forgets us.

Elia was born at 7:15 a.m. after a full night of labor. That sounds grueling, but it really wasn't. Sure, her delivery involved pain and deprived me of sleep. But compared to my prior two labors and deliveries, hers was a dream. I had delivered my boys naturally, which was excruciating. But with Elia, I had an epidural and was actually laughing during delivery. Neal was there to witness the big event, as he had been with both boys. But also present was my sister, who lives in Maryland. She had timed a visit to Chicago with my due date, hoping the two events would coincide, and sure enough, they did.

Events don't often align with our hopes in that way, but everything about Elia's birth defied the odds in our favor. She was, to us, the miracle baby and the answer to hundreds of our prayers. After five years of repeated miscarriages, we had almost given up hope. But here she was—our hope realized in an eight-pound-nine-ounce, twenty-one-inch-long package. We were overcome with gratefulness and joy, and we viewed the difficult journey as nothing compared to its glorious result.

My first miscarriage had occurred about two and a half years after my second son was born. Before then, Neal and I never really worried about my pregnancies going to full term. Both our boys were born without any incident, so we assumed that baby number three would do likewise. Then one morning, I awoke to painful cramps and light bleeding. Within twenty-four hours I had miscarried, and suddenly this baby I had already begun to love was gone. I was sad and confused. But my oldest son, who was then five years old, said something that gave me tremendous peace. The night before I miscarried, we had been sitting around the dinner table when I began cramping and started to cry.

My son asked, "Mom, do all moms cry?"

I responded that yes, probably all moms cry. He asked why I was crying, and I responded honestly, telling him I was afraid I might be losing the baby.

He grew very serious, looked down at his feet for a few seconds, then raised his head and said, "You know, Mom, God's the decider." Those words instantly pierced my soul, and I knew that even if this awful thing happened, God was in control and it would be okay. That assurance helped me accept our loss.

About six months later, I got pregnant again. After eight weeks I miscarried again. Then again. During the seven and a half years between my second son's birth and Elia's birth, I probably miscarried four times. (It's hard to know because two of them may have just been late and heavy periods, but I suspect they were miscarriages.) I also miscarried several times after Elia's birth.

Neal and the boys never gave up hope. For the two years leading up to Elia's birth, the boys earnestly prayed with their daddy for a little sister. Their prayers were so sweet, but I began to believe they were futile. It seemed that God had said no, and we should just accept His decision. I was ready to move on. Pregnancy, even when it ends early, throws your body for a loop. I was tired of riding the ups and downs, physically and emotionally. Neal and I decided we would stop trying to get pregnant, though we wouldn't prevent pregnancy either. Our feelings on birth control had changed over the years, and neither one of us felt right about sterilizing an act that carried such profound spiritual significance. I did, however, sell our baby items at a neighborhood garage sale—except for the crib. It didn't sell, which Neal took as a sign. I just laughed and said we'd sell it at the next garage sale. By the next garage sale, I was pregnant.

Things went well until one morning well into my second trimester. I awoke to the all-too-familiar symptoms. I had a moms' prayer group that morning with close friends. I frantically threw on some clothes, drove to the meeting, and as soon as I sat down, burst into tears. My friends quickly gathered around me and prayed that God would sustain this precious life inside me. My spirit calmed, and I felt assured that God was with me. The symptoms disappeared, and the rest of my pregnancy went smoothly.

Neal and I named Elia after a woman mentioned in a song by the eighties Christian pop band Silverwind. The song told the story of a woman in Communist Russia who refused to submit to authorities' demands that she stop teaching children about Jesus, despite repeatedly being put in prison. When I heard the story as a teenager, I resolved that if I ever had a daughter, I would name her after that brave and godly woman. Nearly two decades later I was able to follow through on that decision.

Hours after Elia was born, Neal brought the boys to visit. My oldest wore a "Big Brother" hat and his little brother wore a "Big Brother" T-shirt. The two of them oozed with excitement as they took turns holding the baby they were convinced they had prayed into existence. My younger son reveled in his new status as an older brother. My oldest kissed Elia's forehead and then exclaimed wide-eyed, "That's the first time I've ever kissed a girl!" From that very first day, the boys have adored their baby sister, and she has adored them. Perhaps due to the large age gap and the unique circumstances of Elia's birth, no hint of sibling rivalry has ever existed between them. To this day, when either of our adult sons comes home, he wants to see Elia first.

Had Elia arrived years earlier, the dynamic between her and her brothers would have been different. Even more profound would have been the dynamic between her and me. Given my prior prejudices against my own gender, I doubt I would have blessed her femininity and likely would have molded her to be like my boys. But God in His wisdom gave me Elia when He knew I was ready to nurture a baby girl. He had prepared me for this task, and I was ready to bless her in the ways that she needed. But I had no idea at the time how Elia would bless me, bringing qualities to life that I never even knew I possessed.

FEMININE BEAUTY REVEALED

With the exception of my conversion to Christ, no circumstance or event in my life has impacted me as much as motherhood. While motherhood initially triggered my insecurities about being a woman, it also developed and affirmed me as a woman more than anything I have ever done. Before my first child was born, I was nervous about whether I would have what it takes to be a good mother. I had many of the stress dreams new moms have, where I would forget to feed my child, for example, or endanger him by doing something outrageous. But I quickly discovered that I possessed all the appropriate instincts necessary to nurture my son. That alone was incredibly reassuring and affirming for me as a woman.

But I was glad God initially gave me boys instead of girls. Since I loved sports and camping and many stereotypically boyish endeavors, I felt competent with boys. And I had a blast raising my two sons. One of them still jokes today about his sense of accomplishment when he finally beat me at a game of one-on-one basketball. He was fourteen at the time. The thought of raising a daughter, though, made me a bit nervous. What if she liked all the stereotypically girly things? What if she wanted to play princess, dance ballet, or create fancy hairdos? Would I be competent to mother a girl like that?

By the time Elia came, though, I had become secure in my feminine identity. And though I still didn't know the first thing about fixing a French braid or doing pirouettes, I was ready to love and nurture a little girl—even if she was different from me. I also had embraced motherhood to a greater degree, as evidenced by my willingness to continue breastfeeding beyond what I viewed to be the obligatory first six months. When six months had expired with both boys, I felt I had done my duty and was done. I was eager to regain some of my freedom and independence, which was hard to do when I had to nurse or express milk every few hours. With Elia, I wasn't in any hurry to escape the demands of motherhood. I had learned how quickly children grow up, and as someone savors every bite of a gourmet meal, I relished those early moments with my infant daughter. She was two years old when I finally stopped nursing.

Elia was a very feminine little girl. She loved dolls and princesses. And while my boys seemed oblivious to what they wore until they became teenagers, Elia took a great interest in her clothes. As early as age two, she would enjoy dressing up and changing her outfits multiple times a day. I had heard mothers of girls describe similar behaviors among their daughters, and how their daughters would create loads of laundry for them to do. Before Elia was born, I remember thinking to myself, *I would never put up with that! What a waste and bother!* But I soon realized that Elia, like many girls, possessed a heightened appreciation for beauty, and for her, trying on new clothes was not an arbitrary way to amuse herself. Dressing up was her way of creating masterpieces. Similarly, she would decorate and redecorate her room as if it were a painter's canvas. I didn't want to inhibit her expression, but took delight in each new creation.

Elia also appreciated beauty in other people. I once picked her up from kindergarten and heard her gush about how beautiful one of her friends was, noting her straight black hair, blue eyes, and pretty smile. I became uncomfortable, thinking perhaps she was picking friends based on their external beauty, rather than appreciating their more substantive features. I asked her if she'd be willing to be friends with someone she didn't think was beautiful. I'll never forget her response, said with such innocence and sincerity: "But Mommy, I've never known anyone who wasn't beautiful!"

That response almost made me cry. I realized watching Elia that her appreciation for beauty was a feminine gift. She saw beauty in everything, even in those things or people others might deem unattractive. And she sought to nurture that beauty, to enhance it and develop it. Certainly some men possess this gift as well. And when balanced by a well-developed masculine, it can be an attractive quality in men too. But this gift seems to reside in a far greater percentage of women, perhaps because the feminine is rooted in the ability to be and to respond. Women stop and smell the roses; we are predisposed to relish goodness and beauty.

As I spent time with Elia, I realized that I possessed this aesthetic appreciation too. In some ways, I had always known that I did. Like most women, I have always enjoyed decorating my house, which is good since Neal has no desire or ability to do so. Similarly, I have strong opinions about what I wear, a characteristic Neal also does not share. In fact, when he and I first met, he was a horrible dresser. After about six months of dating, I bought him new clothes. Reportedly the transformation was so dramatic that his students actually cheered when he first entered the classroom wearing clothes I had bought him.

Yet before Elia, I had never considered my aesthetic sensibilities important or significant. They were fluff—a nice accessory, so to speak, but immaterial compared to the practical things of life. But seeing Elia's aesthetic gifting gave me a much greater appreciation for this feminine quality. I realized more deeply how drab the world would be without the feminine ability to recognize, create, and enhance beauty. I also realized that this ability wasn't merely quaint or cute. It was a feminine expression of the image of God.

This newfound appreciation gave me license to indulge and develop this gift more than I had before. I invested more time in gardening and landscaping; I experimented with new faux painting techniques; I created holiday centerpieces for my dining room. As I did these things, I felt something inside me blossom. I felt I was becoming more authentically me—and quickening a gift that had lain dormant for most of my life.

Elia also helped me better appreciate the feminine capacity to relate to others and to nurture. From the time she was very young, Elia has excelled at relationships. She began talking earlier than any of my children, showing a far greater interest in communication than either of her brothers. And while the boys seemed focused on exploring their physical world, Elia seemed more interested in interacting with other people. She constantly would try to engage the boys, Neal, or me in her play. And when she wasn't interacting with us, she was usually talking to her imaginary friends, having entire conversations with people who didn't exist. On rare occasions, Elia's brothers would interest her in playing with one of their favorite toys, such as blocks. But even then she played completely differently than the boys. They would use the blocks to build skyscrapers and bridges, but Elia would name the blocks and have them talk to each other.

Elia also possessed an astonishing ability to perceive other people's emotions. When she was just eighteen months old, she comforted my mother as she was dying from cancer. When my mother groaned in discomfort, Elia patted her arm and tenderly said, "Oh, oh." As she matured, her ability to sympathize with others only increased. To this day, she is often the first in our family to notice when someone is upset and to respond compassionately.

In Elia I saw the child I might have been, had I grown up under different circumstances. I am eternally grateful for the parents God gave me and the home in which I was raised. But because emotions weren't valued in my home, I learned to manage and mask them. Yet watching Elia, I saw myself in a more transparent and vulnerable form. And I liked what I saw. Her emotional responsiveness made our home a warmer and more inviting place. And once again, being with her drew out something in me. I saw how beautiful and compelling the feminine was in action, and seeing that made me embrace my femininity more tightly than I ever had before. I became more emotionally expressive, more vulnerable, and more responsive. I became more feminine.

These changes were not accidental. God has many purposes for Elia's life, and one of those has been to continue the healing and transformation He began in me. The timing of her birth was too perfect, and the impact of her life and presence too profound, to be coincidence. I believe in the transforming power of God.

A JOURNEY TO TRANSFORMATION

Being a Christian means being a pilgrim, as the German Catholic philosopher Josef Pieper noted in his book *On Hope*. A Christian is not someone who has arrived, he said; he is someone traveling to a new destination. He is someone living in *status viatoris*—the "condition or state of being on the way."[1] Christians today tend to understand a portion of this truth. We understand that we are "on the way" to a new physical location, that we are "foreigners and strangers on earth," as Hebrews 11:13 says, and should be "longing for a better country—a heavenly one" (v. 16 NIV). However, Christians often forget, or even deny, that we are also "on the way" to becoming different people. Inwardly, we are journeying toward becoming like Christ. As the apostle Paul expressed in 2 Corinthians 3:18, "And we all, who with unveiled faces contemplate the Lord's glory, are being transformed into his image with ever-increasing glory" (NIV). Our journey toward Christlikeness will culminate when we see Christ face-to-face. Till then, we are in process. We are progressing toward Christ, but have not yet arrived.

This hope of inner transformation is foundational to the Christian life. Had I not believed that God could and would transform me,

I would have sunk into despair the moment I realized how deeply flawed I was. I also would not have sought His design for my life because I would have doubted that I could ever conform to it. The ancients expressed this hope in our better selves as *magnanimity*—a concept sadly missing in today's culture. As Pieper explained, a magnanimous person is someone who "has the courage to seek what is great and becomes worthy of it." He has a "firm confidence in the highest possibilities of that human nature that God did 'marvelously ennoble and has still more marvelously renewed.'"[2] In other words, a magnanimous person believes in the new creation God is making him or her to be. The Christian woman does not focus on who she is, but rather hopes and trusts in who she is becoming.

Unfortunately, believing in transformation and deliverance is sometimes discouraged today, even within the church. Christian leaders are quick to offer sympathy for a person's ailment or struggle, but not healing. It's as though the gospel is effective only to secure a better afterlife, but is powerless to change us fundamentally. A former colleague of mine summarized this view well in a blog post entitled "The False Hope of Christianity: The Church Has No Business Making Promises Apart from Salvation." He wrote,

> One of the biggest lies churches have led people to believe, intentionally or not, is that when they trust in Jesus, their lives will suddenly become better. All the pain and sorrow of their unsaved days will be washed away with their sins and a beautiful mountaintop experience awaits them where the honeymoon never ends. Of course, it only takes a few years before a lost job, a broken relationship, or the death of a loved one quickly dispels this myth.
>
> But that's when an even bigger lie kicks into high gear: the Christian life has seasons. Pulling from arbitrary biblical imagery,

many will be quick to tell you at a low point in your life that every Christian has seasons of plenty and seasons of famine. There are times you're on top of the mountain and others when you're in the valley of the shadow of death.[3]

My former colleague went on to argue from biblical stories of suffering, like that of the prophet Jeremiah, that fulfillment in this life is a sham. "Some people will never get those mountaintop experiences," he argued. "Some people will be born into abusive homes only to marry an abusive spouse and die a victim but never a victor." Similarly, he said about himself, "I'm certainly not the picture of the victorious life (otherwise known as the evangelical prosperity gospel). People often tell me that my depression and cynicism is just a season, but for all I know, this is the life God has for me." He ended his post equally pessimistic, stating that the purpose God gives each one of us is unique—"And that purpose might suck."[4]

When I read my previous coworker's blog post, I was deeply saddened. I understand and sympathize with his reaction to false promises of deliverance. God does not promise to improve our circumstances. He does not promise to deliver us instantaneously or completely from our sin natures on this side of heaven. This is what Pieper calls presumption. It denies *status viatoris* and presumes the opposite—*status comprehensoris*—the condition or state of having fully comprehended or arrived.[5] Presumption declares a sort of heaven on earth where God erases sin and suffering and the Christian achieves full victory over his own fallen nature. This is the prosperity gospel. And it is the sin that results when "man's desire for security is so exaggerated that it exceeds the bounds of reality."[6]

Even more damaging to our souls than presumption is despair. Despair, according to Pieper, is "a perverse anticipation of the nonfulfillment of hope."[7] It presumes that life will turn out badly for us and for others. It suggests that God has assigned us a purpose that "sucks," and that the diseases of our souls are permanent. It is the appropriate state of being for those who reject Christ and stand condemned. But Jesus said He came to give us abundant life,[8] and for the believer despair is a grievous sin. Like presumption, it also denies *status viatoris*. Instead of embracing the lie that we have arrived, despair embraces the lie that we cannot progress. The Christian is hopelessly stuck in a static state of sin and brokenness. As Pieper wrote, despair is "a decision against Christ" and "a denial of redemption." It is extremely dangerous because "it threatens man's moral existence, for man's self-realization is linked to hope."[9]

Today, many women don't feel like women. Or when we discover what true womanhood is, we may initially react negatively or feel the biblical standard is too high for us to attain. In these moments, it is critical that we choose hope. Hope is the antidote for both presumption and despair. Hope does not deny difficulty, as presumption does, or our remaining brokenness. Yet hope, unlike despair, does not surrender to brokenness either. By embracing pilgrim status, the person who hopes faces difficulty with optimism, trusting that God is working through her to make her more like Jesus. As James 1:2–4 encourages us, we truly can "count it all joy" when we "meet trials of various kinds," knowing that "the testing of [our] faith produces steadfastness." And we can trust that if we "let steadfastness have its full effect," we will eventually "be perfect and complete, lacking in nothing." This is one of the great promises of the gospel. And it has been a persistent driving force in my life. As Paul said in Philippians 3:13–14, I do not consider myself to have arrived, "but one thing I do: forgetting what lies behind and straining forward to what lies ahead, I press on toward the goal for the prize of the upward call of God in

Christ Jesus." I know I am not yet what I will be, but I praise God that I am no longer what I was. And because I know God is faithful, I believe that He is making me into something glorious.

REDEEMED SOULS

When my kids were young, my sister-in-law gave me a series of *Adam Raccoon* books—delightful parables for kids written and illustrated by Glen Keane, former directing animator at Walt Disney Pictures and named a Disney Legend in 2013. Keane's books teach spiritual truths by telling the adventures of a curious raccoon named Adam and a Christ figure, a lion named King Aren. In one book, *Adam Raccoon and the Flying Machine*, King Aren gives Adam a kit for making a flying machine, along with an instruction book and an instructor, a turtle named Earnest. But building the machine takes far more work and time than Adam had anticipated. As he's feeling especially weary of the process, along comes a professor, who announces that following the instruction book is old-fashioned. Now there's a new way: simply do what feels right to you. Delighted with the new plan, Adam tosses the instruction book aside and begins sticking whatever piece onto whichever other part feels right to him. The result is a flying machine that careens out of control and nearly kills Adam.[10]

I remember reading that book to my kids nearly twenty years ago and thinking it aptly described our culture's postmodern approach to constructing identity. We truly have thrown out God's instructions and now are living under the anarchy of our feelings and sin nature. That was true then, but it is even truer today—and not just in culture, but in the church.

In that same twenty years, God has taken me on an incredible journey discovering and progressing toward my true identity—an identity I never could have constructed on my own, or even imagined twenty years ago as I sat crying at a pastors' conference, or enmeshed in a codependent relationship that threatened to wreck me. My identity is something God has revealed to me through His Word and the experience of walking closely with Him. Over these years, He has affirmed the gifts He's given me to lead, teach, and speak. He has also helped me understand how those gifts fit my identity as a woman and how I don't need to suppress my femininity to become my true self. As I have embraced every aspect of my design, I have become more authentically the woman God created me to be. And as I have trusted God through this sometimes-difficult journey, I have come to understand that what He wants for me is greater than what I could imagine for myself. His vision is so much grander than mine. His purpose is so much higher.

I still am realizing only a fraction of the mystery of what it means to be a woman. If together with men we image God, and if God is beyond our comprehension, then I suspect a lifetime is not sufficient to fathom the depths of womanhood or manhood. Nor is a lifetime sufficient to fully achieve the vision God has revealed to us. We remain people in process. I still can easily resort to endless activism and suppress my feminine impulse to be still and listen to the voice of God. And though I am captivated by the beauty of man and woman working together harmoniously to reflect triune love, my husband and I can still clash over petty issues. A slight from a male Christian leader can still inflame me and take weeks to resolve.

But in the midst of the mess, I thank God for His glorious vision and His redemptive process. Though our sin has marred biblical womanhood, it has not erased it. And God, through the power of the cross and His spirit, has given us a means of redeeming what has been lost. What an awesome promise we have that as we pursue Jesus, we are being "transformed into his image with ever-increasing glory."[11] As C. S. Lewis reminds us in his sermon *The Weight of Glory*, "the dullest and most uninteresting person you talk to may one day be a creature which, if you saw it now, you would strongly be tempted to worship. . . . There are no *ordinary* people. You have never talked to a mere mortal."[12]

We are eternal beings either on our way to becoming glorious male and female reflections of God or, as Lewis also warned, becoming "a horror and a corruption."[13] If we follow our culture, the latter will be our destiny. If we follow the cross, we can hardly grasp the beauty of who we will become. Some have speculated about whether or not we retain our genders in heaven. In one sense, there will be no need. When we are standing in God's presence, we will see His actual image and no longer need mere reflections of Him. Plus, as Jesus said, "At the resurrection people will neither marry nor be given in marriage."[14]

But the resurrected Jesus appeared as a man. And my guess is that we women will still appear as women because gender goes beyond our bodies. It reflects an eternal attribute of God, and in heaven we will not cease to reflect God. On the contrary, we will reflect Him perfectly. As Lewis wrote in *Mere Christianity*:

> He will make the feeblest and filthiest of us into a god or god-dess, a dazzling, radiant, immortal creature, pulsating all through with such energy and joy and wisdom and love as we cannot now imagine, a bright stainless mirror which reflects back to God perfectly (though, of course, on a smaller scale) His own boundless power and delight and goodness. The process will be long and in parts very painful, but that is what we are in for.[15]

This promise gives me tremendous hope for the remainder of my journey. It also fills me with hope as I consider my children's futures and helps me, even at my most frustrated, to continue to believe in the church.

We may not arrive at wholeness this side of heaven. Christian men may continue to struggle with the urge to control and to dominate. We women may struggle to escape the false, androgynous vision that culture has ingrained in us and to embrace one from God that's beautifully gendered and true. But if we follow Jesus, we will increasingly find redemption for our feminine and masculine souls. Though the journey may be tough, someday we will see it as the apostle Paul saw his hardships—as nothing compared to the glorious result.[16]

ACKNOWLEDGMENTS

Isaac Newton once famously said "If I have seen further, it is by standing on the shoulders of giants." Certainly, this is true of this book, and many of the "giants" who stimulated my thinking and led me to truth are cited within the chapters of this book. But there are many others, dear brothers and sisters in Christ, without whom this book would never have been written or published.

I am deeply grateful to Church of the Resurrection in Wheaton, Illinois. Because you were faithful to build a sanctuary of transformation, I found healing. You also awakened my imagination to the beauty of men and women serving together in unity. Thanks also to my pastor, Bishop Stewart Ruch, for valuing the feminine on par with the masculine and for blessing the spiritual mothers of the church. And thanks to Stewart's wife, Katherine Ruch, and Rachel Schuchardt who graciously read my rough drafts and offered their wisdom. And thank you Bryan Litfin, professor of theology at the Moody Bible Institute, for graciously reviewing my copy and ensuring it was theologically sound.

Thanks also to Father Eirik and Jeanne Olsen, college classmates and friends for nearly three decades. The Olsens introduced me to healing ministry and over the years have served as an incredible sounding board and constant source of theological and practical insights. So many of the ideas contained in this book were honed during our many conversations together and I can't imagine who I would be today had God not woven our lives together.

I am also indebted to Patrick and Ricki Giersch and Rick and Sabina Dahl, who believed in me and helped me launch as a writer. I will always remember fondly when Patrick asked me "Julie, what do you really want to do?" When I told him I wanted to speak truth to the church and call a generation to holiness, he said "Let's do it!" Without the support of these two couples, my vision would have been nothing but a pipe dream. You gave it wings.

Thanks also to Jeff Hunter, who not only helps me manage my blog, social media, and various projects, but also serves as a constant source of feedback and counsel. Jeff also designed the incredible cover for *Redeeming the Feminine Soul*, which actually makes me hope that people will judge my book by its cover! Thanks also to Daniel Bell, who consulted with me as I built my writing platform. I truly believe God sovereignly connected us for this purpose.

I am also extremely grateful for Lisa Jackson at Alive Literary. Lisa was the first person to hear the proposal for this book and responded with such empathy and enthusiasm that I sensed God was in it. Her constant encouragement and feedback kept me going through the long and arduous process of writing.

Webster Younce at Thomas Nelson served as a fantastic editor. I was a bit skeptical at first about a man editing a book for women. But any doubts I had were quickly dispelled when I received Webb's feedback on the earliest chapters and realized how smart and insightful he is. Thank you, Webb. This book is so much stronger because of your input. Thanks also to the entire team at Thomas Nelson for your incredible support.

I especially thank my family. I knew writing this book would require me to share personal stories and I couldn't have done it without your permission. I was blown away by the responses each of you children gave when I asked. To a person, you said you believed God was going to use this book and encouraged me to go forward. You cared less about our family's image than you did about the ministry of God. For that, I am forever grateful and honored to be your mother.

To my husband Neal, I can't thank you enough. You have been the most supportive and long-suffering spouse any wife could ever hope for. You stuck with me when others might have bolted and you have always believed in my calling as if it was your own. In many ways, it was and is. God called us together and I have experienced His love through you in profound ways. Thank you for the many ways, big and small, that you have laid down your life for me and loved me as Christ loves the church. You have made the intangible tangible and I love you dearly.

Above all, I thank God. I don't fully understand divine providence and election, but I have known from my earliest memories that I am God's daughter and that He loves me. That most precious and fundamental relationship has, does, and always will define me. And it defines womanhood. And it provides the foundation for this book.

ABOUT THE AUTHOR

JULIE ROYS is host of Moody Radio Network's *Up for Debate*, a live, call-in talk show carried on more than 145 stations nationwide. A graduate of Wheaton College and the Medill School of Journalism at Northwestern University, Julie is respected for her ability to tackle difficult conversations with both courage and fairness. Her work has appeared in *World*, *Christianity Today*, the *Federalist*, and the *Christian Post*. She also has appeared on National Public Radio's *Weekend Edition Sunday* and One America News Network's *Tipping Point* and is a sought-after speaker at mega-churches, conferences, and special events. Julie and her husband live in the Chicago area and have three children.

The Genderbread Person v3.3

by it's pronounced METROsexual.com

Gender is one of those things everyone thinks they understand, but most people don't. Like *inception*. Gender isn't binary. It's not either/or. In many cases it's both/and. A bit of this, a dash of that. This tasty little guide is meant to be an appetizer for gender understanding. It's okay if you're hungry for more. In fact, that's the idea.

Identity

Attraction

Sex

Expression

Gender Identity

Woman-ness

Man-ness

How you, in your head, define your gender, based on how much you align (or don't align) with what you understand to be the options for gender.

⊘ Indicates a lack of what's on the right.

Pick a point on both continua in each category to represent your identity; combine all ingredients to form your Gender bread

4 (or infinite) possible pics and label combos

Gender Expression

Feminine

Masculine

The ways you present gender, through your actions, dress, and demeanor, and how those presentations are interpreted based on gender norms.

Biological Sex

Female-ness

Male-ness

The physical sex characteristics you're born with and develop, including genitalia, body shape, voice pitch, body hair, hormones, chromosomes, etc.

Sexually Attracted to

(Women/Females/Femininity)

(Men/Males/Masculinity)

Nobody

Romantically Attracted to

(Women/Females/Femininity)

(Men/Males/Masculinity)

Nobody

In each grouping, circle all that apply to you and pick a point, depicting the aspects of gender toward which you experience attraction.

191

NOTES

INTRODUCTION

1. Crystal Anderson, Katelyn Beaty, Anita Lustrea, Julie Roys, and Morgan Sutter, interview by Melinda Schmidt, "Women: Finding Their Way" parts 1–2, *Bring to Mind*, podcast audio, March 24 and 31, 2014, http://bringtomind.org (site discontinued).

2. Sarah Bessey, *Jesus Feminist: An Invitation to Revisit the Bible's View of Women; Exploring God's Radical Notion that Women Are People, Too* (New York: Howard, 2013).

3. *The Simple Truth about the Gender Pay Gap* (Washington: American Association of University Women, 2016), 3, http://www.aauw.org/files /2016/02/SimpleTruth_Spring2016.pdf.

4. Kurt Bauman and Camille Ryan, "Women Now at the Head of the Class, Lead Men in College Attainment," United States Census Bureau, October 7, 2015, https://www.census.gov/newsroom/blogs /random-samplings/2015/10/women-now-at-the-head-of-the-class -lead-men-in-college-attainment.html.

5. Mark J. Perry, "Women Earned Majority of Doctoral Degrees in 2015 for Seventh Straight Year and Outnumber Men in Grad School 135 to 100," American Enterprise Institute, September 16, 2016, http://www .aei.org/publication/women-earned-majority-of-doctoral-degrees-in-2015- for-7th-straight-year-and-outnumber-men-in-grad-school-134-to-100/.

6. Anna Petherick, "Gains in Women's Rights Haven't Made Women

Happier. Why Is That?" *Guardian*, May 18, 2016, https://www
.theguardian.com/lifeandstyle/2016/may/18/womens-rights-happiness
-wellbeing-gender-gap.

7. Initially, feminists did not embrace abortion and contraception
because they saw motherhood as a means of gaining respect and
finding fulfillment. However, feminists changed their minds about
contraception in the early twentieth century, spurred largely by feminists
who were socialists. These socialist feminists wanted to build a working-
class movement and saw contraception as vital to enabling women to
work outside the home. Other feminists were more reluctant to embrace
abortion, but in the 1960s and 1970s, they, too, began pushing for it
as a way to improve the situation of women. See Linda Gordon, "Why
Nineteenth-Century Feminists Did Not Support 'Birth Control' and
Twentieth-Century Feminists Do: Feminism, Reproduction, and the
Family" in *Rethinking the Family: Some Feminist Questions*, ed. Barrie
Thorne (London: Longman, 1982), 40–52, http://faculty.law.miami.edu
/mcoombs/documents/LGordonBirthControl19thC.pdf.

CHAPTER 1: EXCLUDED FROM THE BOYS CLUB

1. Gen. 3:16 NIV.
2. Jack W. Cottrell, *Gender Roles and the Bible: Creation, the Fall, and
Redemption* (Joplin, MO: College Press, 1994), 126–29.
3. Ibid., 129–30.
4. Gen. 2:7, 18, 21–23.
5. Gen. 2:17.
6. Council on Biblical Manhood and Womanhood, "The Danvers
Statement," June 26, 2007, http://cbmw.org/uncategorized/the-danvers
-statement/.
7. Eph. 5:25.
8. Rusty Lee Thomas, *The Kingdom Leadership Manual: Raising Up
Leaders a Time Like This Demands* (Mustang, OK: Tate Publishing,
2009), 232.
9. Douglas Moo, "What Does It Mean Not to Teach or Have Authority
over Men?" in *Recovering Biblical Manhood and Womanhood: A*

Response to Evangelical Feminism, ed. John Piper and Wayne Grudem (Wheaton, IL: Crossway, 1991), 192.

10. Richard Clark Kroeger and Catherine Clark Kroeger, *I Suffer Not a Woman: Rethinking I Timothy 2:11–15 in Light of Ancient Evidence* (Grand Rapids, MI: Baker, 1992), 79–98.

11. Ibid., 59–76.

12. Gilbert Bilezikian, *Beyond Sex Roles: What the Bible Says About a Woman's Place in Church and Family* (Grand Rapids, MI: Baker, 1985), 134–40.

13. Wayne Grudem, "Does *Kefalh* ('Head') Mean 'Source' or 'Authority Over' in Greek Literature? A Survey of 2,336 Examples," *Trinity Journal* 6, no. 1 (Spring 1985): 38–59, http://www.waynegrudem.com /wp-content/uploads/2012/08/does-kephale-mean-head-or-authority -over.pdf.

14. Andreas J. Köstenberger, Thomas R. Schreiner, and H. Scott Baldwin, eds., *Women in the Church: A Fresh Analysis of 1 Timothy 2:9–15* (Grand Rapids, MI: Baker, 1995), 121–34.

CHAPTER 2: BROKEN, CODEPENDENT, AND SURPRISINGLY FEMININE

1. Name has been changed.

2. Robert Hemfelt, Frank Minirth, and Paul Meier, *Love Is a Choice: The Definitive Book on Letting Go of Unhealthy Relationships* (Nashville: Thomas Nelson, 2003), 5.

3. Ibid., 7–8.

4. Greg E. Dear and Clare M. Roberts, "The Relationships Between Codependency and Femininity and Masculinity," *Sex Roles* 46, no. 5 (March 2002): 159–65.

5. Tab Ballis, "Codependency: The Most Basic Addiction," *Realistic Recovery* (blog), May 20, 2009, https://realisticrecovery.wordpress.com /2009/05/20/codependency-the-most-basic-addiction/.

6. Wendy Kaminer, "Chances Are You're Codependent Too," Books, *New York Times*, February 11, 1990, http://www.nytimes.com/1990/02/11 /books/chances-are-you-re-codependent-too.html?pagewanted=all.

7. Darlene Lancer, *Codependency for Dummies*, 2nd ed. (Hoboken, NJ: John Wiley and Sons, 2015), 34–35.

8. This would have been equally dysfunctional. As Hemfelt, Minirth, and Meier point out, the opposite of codependence isn't independence; it's interdependence—a healthy give-and-take in relationships and balance between independence and dependence. See Hemfelt, Minirth, and Meier, *Love Is a Choice*, 19.

CHAPTER 3: SEX, SEXISM, AND SACRAMENT

1. Paul Farrell, "Anna Duggar, Josh's Wife: Five Fast Facts You Need to Know," *Heavy*, August 20, 2015, http://heavy.com/entertainment /2015/08/anna-josh-duggar-wife-ashley-madison-hack-profile-divorce -facebook-twitter-baby/.

2. Landford Beard, "Josh Duggar Admits Infidelity and Pornography Addiction: 'I Have Been the Biggest Hypocrite Ever,'" *People*, August 20, 2015, http://www.people.com/article/josh-duggar-infidelity-pornography -addiction-statement.

3. "'Josh Duggar Cheated with Me!': Woman Tells All About Their Two Sexual Encounters," *InTouch*, August 26, 2015, http://www.intouch weekly.com/posts/josh-duggar-cheating-affair-mistress-ashley-madison -danica-dillon-68130.

4. Peoplestaff225 [pseud.], "Josh Duggar Paid for an 'Affair Guarantee' on Ashley Madison," *People*, August 21, 2015, http://www.people.com /article/Josh-Duggar-Ashley-Madison-subscription-guaranteed-affair.

5. Harriet Sokmensuer, "Duggar Family Pastor Focuses Sunday Sermon on Infidelity After Ashley Madison Hack: 'We're in a Sexual Epidemic,'" *People*, August 23, 2015, http://people.com/celebrity /duggar-pastor-ronnie-floyd-on-ashley-madison-hack-and-josh-duggar/.

6. "Michelle Duggar's Marriage Advice for Newlyweds," *Duggar Family* (blog), October 8, 2015, http://www.duggarfamily.com/2015/10 /michelle-duggar-s-marriage-advice-for-newlyweds.

7. Julie Roys, "Your Husband's Infidelity Is Not Your Fault: Adultery Comes from a Greedy Heart, Not an Insufficient Wife," Opinion, *Christianity Today*, October 2015, http://www.christianitytoday.com

/women/2015/october/your-husbands-infidelity-is-not-your-fault
.html?paging=off.

8. For a more complete description of complementarianism, see chapter 1, p. 8.

9. Michael Farris, "A Line in the Sand," *Home School Court Report* 30, no. 2 (second quarter, 2014): 6–9, http://www.hslda.org/courtreport /V30N2/HSLDA-2Q-14-CR-EMAG-LOW.pdf.

10. Ibid., 7.

11. Ed Wheat and Gaye Wheat, *Intended for Pleasure: Sex Technique and Sexual Fulfillment in Christian Marriage*, rev. ed. (Grand Rapids, MI: Revell, 1981), 20.

12. Ibid., 22.

13. Christopher West, *Theology of the Body Explained: A Commentary on John Paul II's "Gospel of the Body"* (Herefordshire, UK: Gracewing, 2003), 334–37.

14. Richard M. Hogan and John M. LeVoir, *Covenant of Love: Pope John Paul II on Sexuality, Marriage, and Family in the Modern World*, 2nd ed. (San Francisco: Ignatius, 1992), 44.

15. Pope John Paul II, "Man Enters the World as a Subject of Truth and Love" (general audience, Paul IV Hall, Vatican City, February 20, 1980), quoted in *L'Osservatore Romano English Edition*, February 25, 1980 (Baltimore: Cathedral Foundation), 1.

16. Pope John Paul II, "Mass for Families Neocatechumenal Departing for the Missions" (homily, Porto San Giorgio, December 30, 1988).

17. West, *Theology of the Body Explained*, 15.

18. Leanne Payne, *The Healing Presence: Curing the Soul Through Union with Christ* (Grand Rapids, MI: Hamewith, 1995), 146.

19. Alan W. Jones, *The Drama of the Spiritual Journey: An Exploration of Dante's Comedy* (Atlanta: Catacomb Cassettes of the Episcopal-Radio-TV Foundation, 1980), quoted in ibid., 119.

20. Dennis P. Hollinger, *The Meaning of Sex: Christian Ethics and the Moral Life* (Grand Rapids, MI: Baker, 2009), 72–75.

21. Russell Moore, "Man, Woman, and the Mystery of Christ: A Baptist Perspective" (address, Humanum conference, Vatican City, November 18, 2014), https://www.thegospelcoalition.org/article

/man-woman-and-the-mystery-of-christ-an-evangelical-protestant
-perspective.
22. John 3:16–17.
23. John 14:26.
24. Col. 1:21–22.
25. John 14:26; Rom. 15:16; 1 Cor. 6:19.
26. John 15:26 NIV.
27. John 8:54; When Jesus is baptized and transfigured in Matt. 3:17 and
    Matt. 17:5, some translations say that the Father says that Jesus is the
    Son "in whom I delight" instead of "in whom I am well pleased."
28. 1 Cor. 13:5–7 NIV.
29. Eph. 5:25, 28–30.
30. Moore, "Man, Woman, and the Mystery."
31. West, *Theology of the Body Explained*, 277–281.
32. 1 Cor. 7:8.
33. Council on Biblical Manhood and Womanhood, "Danvers Statement."
34. 1 Tim 3:4–5.
35. 1 Cor. 4:14–15.
36. C. S. Lewis, "Priestesses in the Church?" in *God in the Dock Essays on
    Theology and Ethics*, ed. Walter Hooper (Grand Rapids, MI: Eerdmans,
    2014), 260; previously published as "Notes on the Way," *Time and Tide*
    29 (August 14, 1948): 830–31.
37. C. S. Lewis, "Priestesses in the Church?" in Lesley Walmsley, ed., *C. S.
    Lewis Essay Collection and Other Short Pieces* (London: Fount, 2000), 402.
38. Acts 21:9 KJV.
39. Acts 18:26.
40. Frederica Mathewes-Green, "Women's Ordination," *Frederica.com*
    (blog), January 14, 2007, http://frederica.com/writings/womens
    -ordination.html.

CHAPTER 4: A MAN IN EVERY WOMAN AND A WOMAN IN EVERY MAN

1. Brandan Robertson, "There Are No 'Biblical Men,'" *Patheos*, May 31,
   2015, http://www.patheos.com/blogs/revangelical/2015/05/31/there-are
   -no-biblical-men.html.

2. Rose Angulo, "The Unattainable Proverbs 31 Woman," *She Is More* (blog), http://sheismore.com/the-unattainable-proverbs-31-woman/.

3. Dennis Prager, "The Feminization of America Is Bad for the World," *National Review*, November 3, 2015, http://www.nationalreview.com /article/426473/feminization-america-bad-world-dennis-prager.

4. Robertson, "Biblical Men."

5. Gal. 3:28 NIV.

6. Mark Yarhouse, *Understanding Gender Dysphoria: Navigating Transgender Issues in a Changing Culture* (Downers Grove, IL: IVP Academic, 2015), 16–17.

7. C. S. Lewis, *Perelandra* (New York: Scribner Classics, 1996), 171–172.

8. Leanne Payne, *Crisis in Masculinity* (Grand Rapids, MI: Baker, 1995), 70.

9. Karl Stern, *The Flight from Woman* (Bath, UK: Paragon, 1998), 9.

10. Emil Brunner, *Das Gebot und die Ordnungen* (Tübingen, Ger.: J. C. B. Mohr, 1933), 358, quoted in translation in Paul K. Jewett, *Man as Male and Female* (Grand Rapids, MI: Eerdmans, 1975), 173.

11. Stern, *The Flight from Woman*, 21.

12. Elisabeth Elliot, *The Mark of a Man: Following Christ's Example of Masculinity* (Grand Rapids, MI: Revell, 2009), 55.

13. Ibid., 63.

14. Gen. 2:15.

15. Gen. 3:17–19.

16. Gen. 2:20–22.

17. "Charity, Clarity, and Hope: The Controversy and the Cause of Christ" in *Recovering Biblical Manhood and Womanhood: A Response to Evangelical Feminism*, ed. John Piper and Wayne Grudem (Wheaton, IL: Crossway, 1991), 409.

18. Linda Belleville et al., *Two Views on Women in Ministry*, rev. ed., Counterpoints (Grand Rapids, MI: Zondervan, 2005), 129.

19. John McKinley, "Necessary Allies: God as *Ezer*, Woman as *Ezer*," (address, Evangelical Theological Society, Atlanta, GA, November 17, 2015).

20. Gen. 3:16.

21. Elliot, *Mark of a Man*, 55.

22. C. S. Lewis, *That Hideous Strength: A Modern Fairy-Tale for Grown-Ups* (New York: Scribner, 1996), 316.

23. Wayne Martindale, "C. S. Lewis on Gender Language in the Bible: A Caution," *Touchstone* 1990 (Summer), 5–8, http://touchstonemag .com/archives/article.php?id=04-01-005-f.

24. Payne, *Masculinity*, 86.

25. Ibid.

26. C. S. Lewis to Sister Penelope, Magdalen College, 10 January 1952, in *Letters of C. S. Lewis*, rev. ed., ed. W. H. Lewis (New York: Harvest, 1993), 417.

27. Paul Evdokimov, *Woman and the Salvation of the World*, trans. Anthony Gythiel (Yonkers, NY: St. Vladimir's Seminary, 2011), 138–39.

28. Payne, *Masculinity*, 86.

29. Alice von Hildebrand, *The Privilege of Being a Woman* (Washington, DC: Catholic University of America, 2005), 75–76.

CHAPTER 5: ANDROGYNY, THE NEW MISOGYNY

1. Name has been changed.

2. Larry Crabb, *Men and Women: Enjoying the Difference* (New York: HarperCollins, 1994), 138.

3. Stern, *The Flight from Woman*, 6.

4. Ibid.

5. Jacob Galley, "Stay-at-Home Mothers Through the Years," *Monthly Labor Review* (Bureau of Labor Statistics, September 2014), http://www .bls.gov/opub/mlr/2014/beyond-bls/stay-at-home-mothers-through-the -years.htm.

6. US Census Bureau, "Monthly Microdata," *Current Population Survey*, December 2014, http://dpeaflcio.org/programs-publications /professionals-in-the-workplace/women-in-the-professional-and -technical-labor-force/#_edn1, no longer accessible.

7. Carol Morello, "More Moms Stay at Home, New Research Says," *Washington Post*, April 8, 2014, https://www.washingtonpost.com /local/more-moms-stay-at-home/2014/04/07/feb1f8bc-be91–11e3 -b195-dd0c1174052c_story.html?utm_term=.f8c4ace6a863.

8. Eric Bradner, "U.S. Military Opens Combat Positions to Women," Politics, CNN, December 3, 2015, http://www.cnn.com/2015/12/03 /politics/u-s-military-women-combat-positions/.

9. Dvora Meyers, "Out of Step: Female Gymnasts Used to Be Fantastic Dancers," *Slate*, July 30, 2012, http://www.slate.com/articles/sports /fivering_circus/2012/07/_2012_olympics_gymnastics_female _gymnasts_used_to_be_fantastic_dancers_how_did_the_floor _exercise_get_so_graceless_.html.

10. Melissa Sickmund and Charles Puzzanchera, eds., *Juvenile Offenders and Victims: 2014 National Report* (Pittsburgh: National Center for Juvenile Justice, 2014), 121, http://www.ojjdp.gov/ojstatbb/nr2014 /downloads/chapter5.pdf.

11. Cathy Young, "The CDC's Rape Numbers Are Misleading," Ideas, *Time*, September 17, 2014, http://time.com/3393442/cdc-rape-numbers/.

12. Marguerite Rigoglioso, "Researchers: How Women Can Succeed in the Workplace," *Insights by Stanford Business* (blog), March 1, 2011, https://www.gsb.stanford.edu/insights/researchers-how-women-can -succeed-workplace.

13. Romano Guardini, *The Virtues: On Forms of Moral Life* (Chicago: Regnery, 1967), 6.

14. Gloria Steinem, "The Stage Is Set," *Ms.* (July/August 1982), 77.

CHAPTER 6: BEYOND FEMINISM

1. Alan Rappeport, "Gloria Steinem and Madeleine Albright Rebuke Young Women Backing Bernie Sanders," *New York Times*, February 7, 2016, https://www.nytimes.com/2016/02/08/us/politics/gloria-steinem -madeleine-albright-hillary-clinton-bernie-sanders.html.

2. Madeline Albright, "My Undiplomatic Moment," *New York Times*, February 12, 2016, https://www.nytimes.com/2016/02/13/opinion /madeleine-albright-my-undiplomatic-moment.html.

3. Gloria Steinem's Facebook page, February 7, 2016, https://www .facebook.com/GloriaSteinem/videos/vb.49414682853/1015370033 2282854/?type=2&theater.

4. Lizzie Crocker, "Why Millennial Feminists Don't Like Hillary," *Daily Beast*, October 5, 2015, http://www.thedailybeast.com/articles/2015 /10/05/why-millennial-feminists-don-t-like-hillary.html.

5. See introduction.

6. Hillary Clinton (presidential debate, Thomas and Mack Center,

University of Nevada–Las Vegas, October 19, 2016), quoted in
Claire Chretien, "Breaking: Hillary Defends Partial Birth, Late-Term
Abortion at Beginning of Third Debate," LifeSite, October 19, 2016,
https://www.lifesitenews.com/news/hillary-defends-partial-birth-late
-term-abortion-at-beginning-of-third-deba.

7. Hillary for America, "On Roe v. Wade's Anniversary, One Candidate
Has Lifelong Record of Fighting for Women: Hillary Clinton," The
Briefing, January 22, 2016, https://www.hillaryclinton.com/briefing
/factsheets/2016/01/22/lifelong-record-roe-anniversary/.

8. Katelyn Beaty, "'Jesus Feminists' See Hillary Clinton as a Role
Model. They Just Won't Vote for Her," Acts of Faith, *Washington Post*,
July 20, 2016, https://www.washingtonpost.com/news/acts-of-faith
/wp/2016/07/20/why-some-young-evangelical-women-are-drawn-to
-feminism-and-to-hillary-clinton/.

9. Shawn Boburg, "Enabler or Family Defender? How Hillary Clinton
Responded to Husband's Accusers," Politics, *Washington Post*,
September 28, 2016, https://www.washingtonpost.com/local/enabler
-or-family-defender-how-hillary-clinton-responded-to-husbands
-accusers/2016/09/28/58dad5d4-6fb1-11e6-8533-6b0b0ded0253
_story.html.

10. Hillary Clinton (comment to Bill Clinton Campaign's press corps,
Busy Bee Coffee, Chicago, IL, March 16, 1992), quoted by Jackie
Judd, "Making Hillary Clinton an Issue," *Nightline*, March 26, 1992,
http://www.pbs.org/wgbh/pages/frontline/shows/clinton/etc
/03261992.html.

11. Paul Kengor, "Hillary's Abortion Doctor: Arkansas's Leading Abortionist
Regarded Her as a Christ Figure," *American Spectator*, October 14, 2016,
https://spectator.org/hillarys-abortion-doctor/.

12. "Clinton Hits a New High in Unpopularity: On Par with Trump
among Reg. Voters," ABC News/*Washington Post* Poll, August 31,
2016, http://www.langerresearch.com/wp-content/uploads/1144
-59ClintonTrumpFavorability.pdf.

13. Amanda Hess, "The Dream—and the Myth—of the 'Women's
Vote,'" *New York Times*, November 15, 2016, http://www.nytimes

.com/2016/11/15/magazine/the-dream-and-the-myth-of-the-womens-vote.html.

14. "Gender Gap in 2012 Vote Is Largest in Gallup's History," Gallup, n.d., http://www.gallup.com/poll/158588/gender-gap-2012-vote-largest-gallup-history.aspx.

15. Mary Kassian, *The Feminist Mistake: The Radical Impact of Feminism on Church and Culture* (Wheaton, IL: Crossway, 2005), 17–18.

16. Mary Wollstonecraft, *A Vindication of the Rights of Woman with the Strictures on Political and Moral Subjects* (Dublin: J. Stockdale, 1793), 197.

17. Paul Kengor, *Takedown: From Communists to Progressives; How the Left Has Sabotaged Family and Marriage* (Washington: WND, 2015), 26–27.

18. Simone de Beauvoir, *The Second Sex: A New Translation*, trans. Constance Borde and Sheila Malovany-Chevallier (New York: Alfred A. Knopf, 2009), 63.

19. Ibid., 64.

20. Kengor, *Takedown*, 21.

21. Beauvoir, *Second Sex*, 659.

22. David Horowitz, "Betty Friedan's Secret Communist Past," *Salon*, January 18, 1999, http://www.salon.com/1999/01/18/nc_18horo/.

23. "Humanist Manifest II" (Washington: American Humanist Association, 1973), https://americanhumanist.org/what-is-humanism/manifesto2/.

24. Betty Friedan, *The Feminine Mystique* (New York: W. W. Norton, 2001), 297.

25. Marie Jahoda and Joan Havel, "Psychological Problems of Women in Different Social Roles—A Case History of Problem Formulation in Research," *Educational Record* 36 (1955), 325–33,quoted in ibid., 124, 226.

26. History.com Staff, "Betty Friedan," History.com (2009), http://www.history.com/topics/womens-history/betty-friedan.

27. Kassian, *Feminist Mistake*, 249–50.

28. Ibid., 251.

29. "The Top 50 Books that Have Shaped Evangelicals: Landmark Titles that Changed the Way We Think, Talk, Witness, Worship, and Live,"

Christianity Today, October 6, 2006, http://www.christianitytoday.com
/ct/2006/october/23.51.html.

30. Letha Scanzoni and Nancy Hardesty, *All We're Meant to Be: A Biblical
Approach to Women's Liberation* (Waco, TX; Word, 1974), 110.

31. Mary Stewart Van Leeuwen, *Gender and Grace: Love, Work, and
Parenting in a Changing World* (Downers Grove, IL: IVP Academic,
1990), 185.

32. Katelyn Beaty, *A Woman's Place: A Christian Vision for Your Calling in
the Office, the Home, and the World* (New York: Howard, 2016), 166.

33. Mercer Schuchardt, telephone interview with author, August 23, 2016.

34. "Number of Female Senior Pastors in Protestant Churches Doubles in
Past Decade," Barna Group, September 4, 2009, http://www.barna.com
/research/number-of-female-senior-pastors-in-protestant-churches-doubles
-in-past-decade/.

35. "Fact 2010," Faith Communities Today, http://faithcommunitiestoday
.org/fact-2010.

36. Gretchen Gaebelein Hull, *Equal to Serve: Women and Men in the Church
and Home* (Old Tappan, NJ: Fleming H. Revell, 1987), 121–28.

37. Carolyn McCulley, *Radical Womanhood: Feminine Faith in a Feminist
World* (Chicago: Moody, 2008), 171–77.

38. Nancy Jo Sales, "Tinder and the Dawn of the 'Dating Apocalypse,'"
Vanity Fair, September 2005, http://www.vanityfair.com/culture
/2015/08/tinder-hook-up-culture-end-of-dating.

39. Elizabeth A. Armstrong, Laura Hamilton, and Paula England, "Is
Hooking Up Bad for Young Women?" *Contexts*, August 5, 2010,
https://contexts.org/articles/is-hooking-up-bad-for-young-women/.

40. Sales, "Tinder."

41. Ibid.

42. Ibid.

43. Jennifer Kabbany, "Study: Women Engaged in College Sex Hookups
Experience Depression," *College Fix*, January 16, 2014, http://www
.thecollegefix.com/post/15928/.

44. Joe S. McIlhaney, Jr. and Freda McKissic Bush, *Hooked: New Science on
How Casual Sex Is Affecting Our Children* (Chicago: Northfield, 2008), 43.

45. CDC's National Center for HIV/AIDS, Viral Hepatitis, STD, and TB Prevention, "Reported STDs at Unprecedented High in the U. S.," Centers for Disease Control and Prevention, October 19, 2016, https://www.cdc.gov/nchhstp/newsroom/2016/std-surveillance-report-2015-press-release.html.

46. Hanna Rosin, "Boys on the Side," *Atlantic*, September 2012, http://www.theatlantic.com/magazine/archive/2012/09/boys-on-the-side/309062/.

47. 2 Cor. 5:17; John 1:12; Rom. 6:5–10; Gal. 2:20.

48. "The Gender Spectrum," *Teaching Tolerance* 44 (Summer 2013), http://www.tolerance.org/gender-spectrum.

49. "The Truth About 'Transgender' Bathrooms," Liberty Council, http://www.lc.org/transgender.

50. Tamikka Brents, quoted in Laura Meyers, "Transgender MMA Fighter Destroys Female Opponent," Free Style, *Libertarian Republic*, June 10, 2015, http://thelibertarianrepublic.com/transgender-mma-fighter-destroys-female-opponent/.

51. Andy Bull, "Caster Semenya Wins Olympic Gold but Faces More Scrutiny as IAAF Presses Case," *Guardian*, August 21, 2016, https://www.theguardian.com/sport/2016/aug/21/caster-semenya-wins-gold-but-faces-scrutiny.

52. Jos Truitt, "The Olympic Games Are Obsessed with Policing Femininity," *Feministing*, http://feministing.com/2012/06/14/the-olympic-games-are-obsessed-with-policing-femininity/.

53. HRC staff, "Openly Transgender Athletes Notably Absent from Olympic Roster," Human Rights Campaign blog, August 11, 2016, http://www.hrc.org/blog/openly-transgender-athletes-notably-absent-from-olympic-roster.

54. Phil. 2:15 NIV.

55. McIlhaney and Bush, *Hooked*, 36–37.

56. Katherine Ruch, "An Elegy for Gender? The Encroachment of Androgyny," *Still Point of the Turning World* (blog), September 26, 2015, http://worldstillpoint.blogspot.com/2015/09/an-elegy-for-gender-encroachment-of.html.

57. Chris Chambers, "Mothers Still Perceived as Having More Dominant Influence Than Fathers, but Dads Don't Seem to Mind," Gallup, June 16, 2000, http://www.gallup.com/poll/2812/mothers-still -perceived-having-more-dominant-influence-than-fathers.aspx.

58. Judg. 4:4–24.

59. Although this quote is often attributed to Gloria Steinem, it is Irina Dunn's 1970 paraphrase of Vique's Law. Lea Carpenter, "Lesson 21: Gloria Steinem's Aphorisms; Fish, Power, Love, Bunnies, and Life," Big Think, http://bigthink.com/english-lessons/lesson-21-gloria-steinems -aphorisms-fish-power-love-bunnies-and-life.

60. "Table C8: Poverty Status, Food Stamp Receipt, and Public Assistance for Children Under Eighteen Years by Selected Characteristics," United States Census Bureau (2014), http://www.census.gov/hhes /families/data/cps2014C.html.

61. Isabel Sawhill, "Twenty Years Later, It Turns out Dan Quayle Was Right About Murphy Brown and Unmarried Moms," Opinions, *Washington Post*, May 25, 2012, https://www.washingtonpost.com /opinions/20-years-later-it-turns-out-dan-quayle-was-right-about -murphy-brown-and-unmarried-moms/2012/05/25/gJQAsNCJqU _story.html?utm_term=.86ee3f90089b.

62. John Cairney et al., "Stress, Social Support and Depression in Single and Married Mothers," *Social Psychiatry and Psychiatric Epidemiology* 38, no. 8 (August 2003): 442–49, https://www.ncbi.nlm.nih.gov /pubmed/12910340.

CHAPTER 7: GENDER CONSTRUCTION AND CONFUSION

1. John 14:6.

2. Nancy Pearcey, *Finding Truth: Five Principles for Unmasking Atheism, Secularism, and Other God Substitutes* (Colorado Springs: David C. Cook, 2015), 63, 150.

3. Ibid.

4. Stanley J. Grenz, *A Primer on Postmodernism* (Grand Rapids, MI: Eerdmans, 1996), 8.

5. Richard Rorty, *Philosphy and Social Hope* (New York: Penguin, 1999).

6. "Understanding Gender," Gender Spectrum, https://www.gender spectrum.org/quick-links/understanding-gender/.

7. Joy D'Souza, "What Is the Expanded LGBT Acronym? And What Does It Stand For?" *Huffington Post*, June 27, 2016, http://www .huffingtonpost.ca/2016/06/27/entire-lgbt-acronym_n_10616392.html.

8. Sam Killermann, *The Social Justice Advocate's Handbook: A Guide to Gender* (Austin: Impetus, 2013), 107.

9. Kendra Cherry, "What Is Gender Schema Theory?" VeryWell, May 9, 2016, https://www.verywell.com/what-is-gender-schema-theory-2795205.

10. Killermann, *The Social Justice Advocate's Handbook*, 57–59.

11. Sue Ellin Browder, "Kinsey's Secret: The Phony Science of the Sexual Revolution," CatholicCulture.org, 2004, https://www.catholicculture .org/culture/library/view.cfm?recnum=6036.

12. "Understanding Gender."

13. Anne Fausto-Sterling et al., "How Sexually Dimorphic Are We? Review and Synthesis," *American Journal of Human Biology* 12 (2000): 151–66.

14. Leonard Sax, "How Common Is Intersex? A Response to Anne Fausto -Sterling," *Journal of Sex Research* 39, no. 3 (August 2002): 174–78, https://www.jstor.org/stable/3813612?seq=1#page_scan_tab_contents.

15. Pew Research Center, "Support for Same-Sex Marriage at Record High, but Key Segments Remain Opposed," June 2015, 17, http://www .people-press.org/files/2015/06/6-8-15-Same-sex-marriage-release1.pdf.

16. "Global Christian Attitudes Towards Transgenderism 'Softening,' Study Suggests," St. John's College, University of Cambridge, January 12, 2015, http://www.cam.ac.uk/research/news/global-christian-attitudes -towards-transgenderism-softening-study-suggests.

17. Duncan Dormor, interview by Antony Bushfield, *News Hour*, Premier Christian Radio, December 2, 2015.

18. Matthew Vines, *God and the Gay Christian: The Biblical Case in Support of Same-Sex Relationships* (London: Convergent, 2014), 95, 103.

19. Weston Gentry, "Exodus International's Alan Chambers Accused of Antinomian Theology," *Christianity Today*, July 12, 2012, http:// www.christianitytoday.com/ct/2012/julyweb-only/alan-chambers -accused-of-antinomian-theology.html.

20. Lou Chibbaro Jr., "Former 'Ex-gay' Leader to March in Pride Parade," *Washington Blade*, June 9, 2016, http://www.washingtonblade .com/2016/06/09/former-ex-gay-leader-to-march-in-pride-parade/.

21. Restored Hope Network, http://restoredhopenetwork.org/.

22. Stanton L. Jones, "Same-Sex Science: The Social Sciences Cannot Settle the Moral Status of Homosexuality," *First Things* (February 2012), https://www.firstthings.com/article/2012/02/same-sex-science.

23. Matthew Vines, *God and the Gay Christian: The Biblical Case in Support of Same-Sex Relationships* (London: Convergent Books, 2014).

24. Sidney D. Fowler, "What Matters: We Listen for a Still-Speaking God," United Church of Christ, http://www.ucc.org/vitality_what -matters_we-listen-for-a.

25. Vines, *God and the Gay Christian*, 105.

26. Francis Mark Mondimore, *A Natural History of Homosexuality* (Baltimore: Johns Hopkins, 1996).

27. Michel Foucault, *The History of Sexuality*, vol. 1, trans. Robert Hurley (New York: Random House, 1980), 43.

28. This is explained in detail in chapter 3.

29. Cecilia Dhejne et al., "Long-Term Follow-Up of Transsexual Persons Undergoing Sex Reassignment Surgery: Cohort Study in Sweden," *PLOS ONE* 6, no. 2 (February 22, 2011), http://journals.plos.org /plosone/article?id=10.1371/journal.pone.0016885.

30. John 14:6 NIV.

31. Matt. 7:13 NIV.

CHAPTER 8: REDEMPTIVE SUFFERING

1. 2 Kings 5:1–14.

2. Linda Dillow and Juli Slattery, *Surprised by the Healer: Embracing Hope for Your Broken Story* (Chicago: Moody, 2016), 7, 10.

3. Michelle C. Black et al., *The National Intimate Partner and Sexual Violence Survey (NISVS): 2010 Summary Report* (Atlanta, GA: National Center for Injury Prevention and Control, Centers for Disease Control and Prevention, 2011), http://www.cdc.gov /violenceprevention/pdf/NISVS_Report2010-a.pdf.

4. B. O. Rothbaum et al., "A Prospective Examination of Post-Traumatic Stress Disorder in Rape Victims," *Journal of Traumatic Stress* 5 (1992): 455–75.

5. B. O. Rothbaum and E. B. Foa, "Subtypes of Posttraumatic Stress Disorder and Duration of Symptoms," in J. R. T. Davidson and E. B. Foa, eds., *Posttraumatic Stress Disorder: DSM-IV and Beyond* (Washington: American Psychiatric Press, 1992), 23–36.

6. D. G. Kilpatrick et al., "Rape in America: A Report to the Nation" (Arlington, VA: National Victim Center and Medical University of South Carolina, 1992), http://www.victimsofcrime.org/docs /reports%20and%20studies/rape-in-america.pdf?sfvrsn=0.

7. Callie Marie Rennison, "Rape and Sexual Assault: Reporting to Police and Medical Attention, 1992–2000," August 2002, https://www.bjs .gov/content/pub/pdf/rsarp00.pdf.

8. Dillow and Slattery, *Surprised by the Healer*, 7.

9. Rachel K. Jones, Lawrence B. Finer, and Susheela Singh, *Characteristics of U. S. Abortion Patients, 2008* (New York: Guttmacher Institute, 2010), 9, https://www.guttmacher.org/sites/default/files/report_pdf/us -abortion-patients.pdf.

10. "Abortion: Its Effect on Men" in *Women's Health After Abortion: The Medical and Psychological Evidence* (Toronto: deVeber Institute for Bioethics and Social Research, 2014), 249–50, http://www.deveber .org/text/chapters/Chap16.pdf.

11. Vincent M. Rue et al., "Induced Abortion and Traumatic Stress: A Preliminary Comparison of American and Russian Women," *Medical Science Monitor* 10, no. 10 (2004): SR5–16, http://www.medscimonit .com/download/index/idArt/11784.

12. Elliot Institute, "Abortion Risks: A List of Major Psychological Complications Related to Abortion," http://afterabortion.org/2011 /abortion-risks-a-list-of-major-psychological-complications-related-to -abortion/.

13. Julie Roys, "The Secret Shame of Abortion in the Church," Opinion, *Christianity Today*, February 2015, http://www.christianitytoday.com /women/2015/february/secret-shame-of-abortion-in-church.html?start=3.

14. "ChristiaNet Poll Finds that Evangelicals Are Addicted to Porn," Marketwired, August 7, 2006, http://www.marketwired.com/press -release/christianet-poll-finds-that-evangelicals-are-addicted-to -porn-703951.htm.

15. K. P. Mark et al., "Infidelity in Heterosexual Couples: Demographic, Interpersonal, and Personality-Related Predictors of Extradyadic Sex," *Archives of Sexual Behavior* 40, no. 5 (October 2011): 971–82, http:// www.ncbi.nlm.nih.gov/pubmed/21667234.

16. Frank Bass, "Cheating Wives Narrowed Infidelity Gap over Two Decades," Bloomberg, July 1, 2013, http://www.bloomberg.com/news /articles/2013–07–02/cheating-wives-narrowed-infidelity-gap-over -two-decades.

17. "Female Gamblers Fact Sheet," National Council on Problem Gambling, http://www.ncpgambling.org/files/WOMEN_GAMBLERS _FACTS.pdf.

18. "Women and Alcoholism," Promises Treatment Centers, April 14, 2010, https://www.promises.com/articles/women-and-alcohol/women -and-alcoholism-2/.

19. NEDA, "Get the Facts on Eating Disorders," National Eating Disorders Association, https://www.nationaleatingdisorders.org /get-facts-eating-disorders.

20. "Self-Injury (Cutting, Self-Harm or Self-Mutilation)," Mental Health America, http://www.mentalhealthamerica.net/self-injury.

21. Stephen Seamands, *Wounds That Heal: Bringing Our Hurts to the Cross* (Downers Grove, IL: IVP Books, 2003), 118–19.

22. Juli Slattery, interview by Julie Roys, "Seeking Truth—Reclaiming God's Design for Human Sexuality," *Seeking Truth with Julie Roys*, podcast audio, August 22, 2016, http://julieroys.com/seeking -truth-sexuality/.

23. Rom. 8:28.

24. John 12:24.

25. Chuck Colson, "Suffering and Redemption," *Christian Post*, February 9, 2008, http://www.christianpost.com/news/suffering-and-redemption -31131/.

26. Seamands, *Wounds*, 113.
27. Matt. 16:24 NIV.
28. Isa. 53:3.
29. Luke 4:1–13.
30. Matt. 26:39.
31. George Wootan, "Mother-Baby Separation," Peaceful Parenting, July 13, 2010, http://www.drmomma.org/2010/07/mother-toddler -separation.html.
32. Seamands, *Wounds That Heal*, 128.
33. Slattery, interview, "Seeking Truth."
34. Matt. 7:13–14 NIV.
35. Robert Frost, "The Road Not Taken," *Mountain Interval* (New York: Henry Holt, 1916), 9.

CHAPTER 9: MARGINALIZING MOTHERHOOD

1. Shauna Niequist, "What My Mother Taught Me" (Q Nashville, Nashville, Tennessee, on April 24, 2014), YouTube video, 17:58, posted by QIdeas.org, May 9, 2014, https://www.youtube.com /watch?v=dIzgyW95grc.
2. Ibid.
3. Ibid.
4. Lonnae O'Neal Parker, "Four Years Later, Feminists Split by Michelle Obama's 'Work' as First Lady," *Washington Post*, January 18, 2013, https://www.washingtonpost.com/lifestyle/style/feminists-split-by -michelle-obamas-work-as-first-lady/2013/01/18/be3d636e-5e5e-11e2 -9940-6fc488f3fecd_story.html?utm_term=.604ff681d8a3.
5. Emily Bazelon, "Dispatches from the Democratic National Convention: It Was a Great Speech. But Did Michelle Obama Sell Herself Short?" Politics, *Slate*, September 5, 2012, http://www .slate.com/articles/news_and_politics/the_breakfast_table/features /2012/_2012_democratic_national_convention/michelle_obama _s_speech_was_an_enormous_success_but_it_didn_t_say_enough _for_working_moms_.html.
6. Friedan, *Feminist Mystique*, 423.

7. Jonathan Merritt, "The Conservative, Christian Case for Working Women," *Atlantic*, July 5, 2016, http://www.theatlantic.com/politics /archive/2016/07/the-conservative-christian-case-for-working-women /490025/.

8. Gen. 1:28 NIV.

9. Beaty, *A Woman's Place*, 66.

10. Ibid., 98–111.

11. Katelyn Beaty, "Why We Still Need 'The Feminine Mystique': The Surprising Christian Anthropology at the Heart of Betty Friedan's Book," Books and Culture, July 2014, http://www.booksandculture .com/articles/webexclusives/2014/july/why-we-still-need-feminine -mystique.html.

12. Ibid.

13. Sarah Treleaven, "Inside the Growing Movement of Women Who Wish They'd Never Had Kids," *Marie Claire*, September 28, 2016, http://www.marieclaire.com/culture/a22189/i-regret-having-kids/.

14. Jennifer Hartline, "Baby, You Stole the Life I Wanted," *The Stream*, October 5, 2016, https://stream.org/baby-stole-life-wanted/.

15. West, *Theology of the Body Explained*, 121.

16. Luke 11:27 NIV.

17. 1 Tim. 5:9–10 NIV.

18. 2 Tim. 1:5 NIV.

19. John F. MacArthur, *Successful Christian Parenting* (Nashville: Thomas Nelson, 1999), 194.

20. William Ross Wallace, "The Hand That Rocks the Cradle," quoted in *World's Renowned Authors: And Their Grand Masterpieces of Poetry and Prose*, ed. Henry Davenport Northrup (Kansas City, MO: Topeka Books, 1902), 454.

21. Theodore Roosevelt, "To the Delegates to the First International Congress in America on the Welfare of the Child at the White House" (address, White House, Washington, DC, March 10, 1908), http:// www.theodore-roosevelt.com/images/research/txtspeeches/281.txt.

22. Candice Watters, quoted in Julie Roys, "Moms in Crisis: Two Views," *Julie Roys* (blog), January 28, 2015, http://julieroys.com/moms -in-crisis-two-views/.

23. Julia Mateer, "Discover Your God-Given Calling: Find Your Passion and Put It into Action," *Christianity Today*, February 7, 2013, http://www .christianitytoday.com/gifted-for-leadership/2013/february/discover-your -god-given-calling.html?.

24. Matt. 10:39.

25. Caroline Beaton, "What No One Told Me About Following My Passion," Under 30, *Forbes*, June 29, 2016, http://www.forbes.com /sites/carolinebeaton/2016/06/29/what-no-one-told-me-about- following-my-passion/#155f128124c4.

26. Marc-André K. Lafrenière et al., "On the Relation Between Performance and Life Satisfaction: The Moderating Role of Passion," *Self and Identity* 11, no. 4 (October 25, 2011): 516–530, http://www .tandfonline.com/doi/abs/10.1080/15298868.2011.616000.

27. Terri Trespicio, "Stop Searching for Your Passion," YouTube video, 10:47, from an address at TEDx event in Kansas City, Kansas, on September 14, 2015, posted by TEDx Talks, September 15, 2015, https://www.youtube.com/watch?v=6MBaFL7sCb8.

28. Roy F. Baumeister et al., "Some Key Differences between a Happy Life and a Meaningful Life," *Journal of Positive Psychology* 8, no. 6 (August 2013): 505–16, https://www.gsb.stanford.edu/faculty-research /publications/some-key-differences-between-happy-life-meaningful-life.

29. Beaton, "What No One Told Me."

30. Matt. 16:25 NIV.

31. Gilbert K. Chesterton, *What's Wrong with the World* (New York: Dodd, Mead, 1912), 164–65.

32. Robert M. Lewis, *The New Eve: Choosing God's Best for Your Life* (Nashville: B & H, 2008), 101.

33. Danielle Crittenden, *What Our Mothers Didn't Tell Us: Why Happiness Eludes the Modern Woman* (New York: Simon and Schuster, 1999), 22, 60.

34. Rebecca Adams, "Why Men May Not Try to 'Have It All' the Same Way Women Do," *Huffington Post*, December 8, 2014, http://www .huffingtonpost.com/2014/12/08/women-success_n_6219586.html.

35. Aimee Picchi, "These Women Can't Find Enough Marriageable Men," Moneywatch, CBS.com, September 24, 2015, http://www.cbsnews.com /news/these-women-cant-find-enough-marriageable-men/.

36. Darrow L. Miller, *Nurturing the Nations: Reclaiming the Dignity of Women in Building Healthy Cultures* (Colorado Springs: Paternoster Publishing, 2007), 259–61.
37. Ibid., 245.
38. "Learn More. Questions and Answers About: 'The New Economic Reality: Demographic Winter:' Parts 1 and 2," *New Economic Reality* (blog), n.d., http://www.theneweconomicreality.com/learn.html.
39. Miller, *Nurturing the Nations*, 251.
40. Crittenden, *What Our Mothers Didn't Tell Us*, 123.
41. Shauna Niequist, *Present over Perfect: Leaving Behind Frantic for a Simpler, More Soulful Way of Living* (Grand Rapids, MI: Zondervan, 2016), 44–46.
42. Watters, quoted in Roys, "Moms in Crisis."

CHAPTER 10: THE GLORIOUS BECOMING

1. Josef Pieper, *On Hope* (San Francisco: Ignatius, 1986), 11–12.
2. Aquinas, *Summa Theologiae*, ed. Thomas Gilby (New York: McGraw Hill, 1964–1981), 2.2.129.3, reply to objection 4, quoted in ibid., 28.
3. Alex Bersin, "The False Hope of Christianity," *The Christian Skeptic* (blog), December 1, 2015, http://www.alexbersin.com/2015/12/the-false-hope-of-christianity.html.
4. Ibid.
5. Pieper, *On Hope*, 11, 65–68.
6. Ibid., 67.
7. Ibid., 47.
8. John 10:10.
9. Pieper, *On Hope*, 50–52.
10. Glen Keane, *Adam Raccoon and the Flying Machine* (Colorado Springs: Chariot Victor, 1997).
11. 2 Cor. 3:18 NIV.
12. C. S. Lewis, *The Weight of Glory and Other Addresses* (New York: HarperOne, 2009), 45–46.
13. Ibid., 45.
14. Matt. 22:30 NIV.
15. C. S. Lewis, *Mere Christianity*, rev. ed. (New York: MacMillan, 1952), 205–6.
16. Rom. 8:18.